WOMEN WHO HIKE

Walking with America's
Most Inspiring Adventurers

HEATHER BALOGH ROCHFORT

Guilford, Connecticut

FALCON®

An imprint of The Rowman & Littlefield Publishing Group, Inc.
4501 Forbes Blvd., Ste. 200
Lanham, MD 20706
www.rowman.com
Falcon and FalconGuides are registered trademarks and Make Adventure Your Story
is a trademark of The Rowman & Littlefield Publishing Group, Inc.

Distributed by NATIONAL BOOK NETWORK
Copyright © 2019 Heather Balogh Rochfort
Maps by The Rowman & Littlefield Publishing Group, Inc.

British Library Cataloguing-in-Publication Information available
Library of Congress Cataloging-in-Publication Data available

ISBN 978-1-4930-3713-1 (paperback)
ISBN 978-1-4930-3714-8 (e-book)

∞™ The paper used in this publication meets the minimum requirements of American National Standard for Information Sciences—Permanence of Paper for Printed
Library Materials, ANSI/NISO Z39.48-1992.

Printed in the United States of America

The author and The Rowman & Littlefield Publishing Group, Inc., assume no
liability for accidents happening to, or injuries sustained by, readers who engage
in the activities described in this book.

Contents

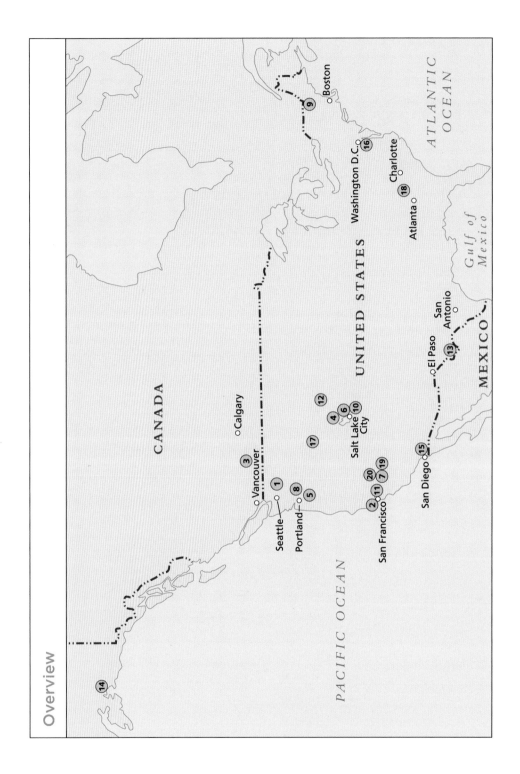

Foreword

When we hike, we're doing more than moving forward through outdoor spaces with our bodies. Hiking is how we experience ourselves. In a world grown claustrophobic by our crowded digital lives, hiking brings us back to earth. It slows us down, connects us to profound spirituality, gives us room to grow bigger and feel small. The trails we seek are classrooms, fresh air emporiums peddling life lessons and introspections.

Hiking brings us together. That's how I met Heather Balogh Rochfort—on a hike down to Havasu Falls in Arizona. We arrived in Sedona as strangers on a press trip, but as we ambled on red clay trails and down into the branches of the Grand Canyon, we became friends. Heather has infectious warmth. Maybe it was just the blanket of heat radiating from both the earth and bluebird sky, but something about hiking with Heather reminds you how good it feels to be alive.

As most of us are on our first big outdoor ventures, I was ill prepared that trip down to Havasu Falls. It was my first overnight hike: twenty-five miles over three days, six travertine waterfalls, a dozen hikers of varying athletic abilities, and one leech-infested swimming hole. A freshly transplanted Floridian flatlander meeting elevation gains for the first time, I didn't know how to pace myself, layer myself, or brace my body for what I was about to ask of it. On the last day, I awoke before dawn to start down the trail hours before anyone else, and was still the very last hiker to reach the trailhead terminus. My time in that canyon left me blistered, dehydrated, and a wholly different person than the human I was when my boots first hit the trail. It was one of the best hikes of my life.

So why do women hike?

Why does anyone, really?

We hike to see what's out there. We hike to heal, to fall apart, to find and lose ourselves on the trail. We hike because our mothers did, because our sisters do, because that's what we want our daughters to do. We hike to experience the earth at a human-powered pace.

We hike for the same reasons you're reading this book: to discover and be inspired, or to experience something new, or to return to the comfort of a familiar place. We hike to see other humans that look like us out there on the trails, too—to share fresh air with old friends and mountaintop snacks with strangers.

Heather boasts an impressive résumé , making her the type of person qualified to write an anthology of badass women who pursue hikes, but it isn't her penmanship of *Backpacking 101* or her work as an adaptive youth ski instructor that offers the true depth of Heather's outdoor expertise. It's the way she moves through the mountains. She feels each step of her feet padding through the woods. She remembers to revel in the smell of wet earth, the sound of windy aspens flittering like tambourine zills, the frigid surprise of alpine water. She sees the prowess of towering mountain frames, and the intricacies of tiny wildflower petals.

She uses those mountain moments to shape her life, to fortify who she is and what she wants to share with the world around her. It's something we should all strive to do. To move through all instances in life as if we were hiking along a trail. The women featured in this book embody that way of living too. Hiking isn't what they do; it's the bedrock of who they are.

The *Women Who Hike* are a cross-section of the many definitions of a hiker. You'll meet women defying the traditional idea of what an outdoorswoman looks like: mothers who hike to raise the next generation, big mountain trekkers who founded their own businesses, indigenous women reconnecting to their ancestors through the land.

You'll find me in this book too, celebrating my local Utah trails. Some paths in this book are high summit peaks, tucked deep into the wilderness. Some, like mine, have trailheads that climb into the mountains from urban parking lots. The beauty of hiking is that it can happen anywhere. You can go for a hike in forests miles from another human, or you can thru-hike a metropolitan city. Hiking is what you make it.

And that 2012 hike to Havasu Falls? That was the trail that introduced Heather Balogh to me, and to William Rochfort. As we all marched through the ruddy desert, flitting along sandstone boulders and climbing through wet tunnels, a little love story sparked between those two. Moments cultivated on the trail led to love letters, a first date, a Colorado countryside wedding—I caught the bouquet, *thank you very much*—and a daughter named Liliana. All because we went for a hike.

Going for a hike is always a good idea. In your backyard, through the backcountry—whatever it is you're looking for, you'll find it out on the trails. Hiking is a catalyst for the rest of your life. You'll find a bit of that magic in these pages too.

—Katie Boué

Acknowledgments

There are so many people to thank for the creation of this project that I struggle to know where to begin! First, I'd be remiss if I didn't express my utter gratitude and respect for the twenty women featured in these pages. Not only did they use their limited free time to speak with me and pull together photos, but these ladies have also spent a lifetime breaking down glass walls and showing the world what it looks like to be a strong female in the outdoor industry. It's not easy to forge your own trail but these women do it with style and class, regardless of whether they even realize it. I respect each and every one of the women highlighted in these pages and I sincerely enjoyed learning about their journeys.

Erica deserves a gigantic thank you for all of her dedication and help. Without her assistance, exquisite computer skills, and attention to detail, I suspect I would be in a lot of trouble.

I'd also like to thank my husband for his eternal patience and support for all of my crazy ideas. I truly don't think I could do it without his unwavering commitment and I'm so thankful to have him by my side for all of life's adventures. You are my rock; you are my everything.

A special thanks goes to my parents and little sister for filling my formative years with exceptionally long nature walks that pulled double duty as hikes. While I (really) didn't appreciate those at the time, I'm convinced those early days were the stepping stones that led me to grander adventures.

Finally, I'd like to thank our baby girl Liliana, even though she can't read just yet. Her zest for life and infectious enthusiasm make every day better than the last. I thank my lucky stars every day that she chose me to be her mother, and I can only hope she grows up to be as strong, kind, and fierce as the women highlighted in these pages.

Introduction

In 2001, I was a broke college student living in Boulder, Colorado. I'd recently taken up mountaineering and although I certainly didn't have the funding for fancy gear, I saved up enough cash via my work study job to buy my first pair of legitimate mountaineering boots. But the joke was on me; after visiting every outdoor goods store in the city, I realized that no one stocked female mountaineering boots. I was baffled. This was Boulder, arguably the outdoor mecca of the country. If I couldn't find mountaineering boots here, I surely couldn't find them anywhere.

In the end, I swallowed my pride in the name of practicality and bought a pair of men's size six demo boots from the only shop in town carrying such absurdly small men's footwear. Thankfully, no one in town had actually tested them out since they were too tiny for most men, but my stomach churned at the purchase. I didn't have any options in brands or styles and the fit didn't really matter; I could take this single pair of demo boots or leave them.

Almost two decades later and that memory still stands vividly in my mind. I won't pretend to be a pioneer in the outdoor industry; at the tender age of 37, that would be arrogant and presumptuous. But I've been around long enough to remember the male-dominated trails of my early outdoor years. And while I'm thankful for all of the kind and generous men who showed me the way, I am even more grateful for the few-and-far-between women I met during my own personal journey. We've come a long way since then but the celebration of outdoor women is a relatively new occurrence.

The twenty women highlighted in the following pages epitomize the modern outdoor woman. From immigrants to professional athletes, CEOs of outdoor companies to editors of magazines, filmmakers to outdoor advocates, these women are the multifaceted future of the industry. And each one loves to hike, whatever that individually means to her.

Each woman has indicated her best-loved trail in the country. For some, the hike is simply a favorite thanks to the aesthetic beauty of the natural surroundings, but for many others, the trails enclosed in this book hold special meaning. As you tackle the hikes suggested in this guidebook, remember the individual stories that correspond to the trail.

Happy trails, my friends. May you find whatever you're searching for out there.

—Heather Balogh Rochfort

How to Use This Guide

This guidebook is by no means a comprehensive resource and it certainly cannot answer every single question you have about your planned hike. But then again, that is the beauty of hiking: the mystery you uncover around every bend in the trail.

Each woman highlighted in this book chose her favorite trail, which means you will find a wide variety of treks. Some hikes are as short as a mile or two, easily accessible for families with small children or hikers looking to get out and stretch their legs. On the other end, some of the featured routes are long hauls of 100 miles that call for planning, navigation, and outdoor experience. This book is a choose your own adventure of hiking fun, but it is your responsibility to choose a trail best suited to your abilities.

Included with each route description are helpful pieces of information such as average hiking time, distance and elevation gain, trails used, and special considerations. Driving directions and GPS coordinates are provided for the trailheads to each hike as well. Finally, a basic map is provided with trails, providing distances and key points along the route. Each hiker is different and I understand that hiking times will vary widely from person to person, so I tried to estimate ballpark timeframes as best as possible.

TYPES OF TRIPS

There are three categories of hikes you will see in this book:

Out-and-Back: This means you will hike to a specific destination and then turn around to retrace your steps back to the trailhead.

Loop: This type of hike begins and ends at the same location with minimal retracing of your steps. If you look at the corresponding map, you will see that your route follows a loop-shaped pattern. In at least one instance, you will see the term "lollipop loop" used to describe a trail. This means you will hike for a distance, then complete a loop before retracing your steps back to the trailhead.

Point-to-Point: This type of hike is a one-way journey, meaning you begin at one trailhead and conclude at another. Frequently, this calls for a car shuttle or another means of transportation to return you from whence you came.

DIFFICULTY RATINGS

It is difficult to standardize ratings of trail difficulty since it is largely subjective and depends on the individual and her fitness levels. That said, I tried to standardize each hike as best as I could to help prepare for your adventures. In doing so, I used three categorizations:

Easy trails are suitable for any hiker. This includes families with children, the elderly, and anyone who is hoping to learn more about hiking. Elevation gain is minimal and you will encounter very few trail hazards. Navigation is almost nonexistent and you will never have to go off-trail.

Moderate trails are suitable for any hiker who has some experience outdoors and on the trail. You will need an average fitness level to complete a moderate hike and specific sections may still challenge you. Occasional route-finding may be required and you can expect elevation gain to range from 1,000–2000 feet over the course of the trail.

Strenuous trails are the most challenging hikes you will find in this book. These are meant for very experienced outdoorists who have a high level of fitness and confidence in their abilities. The trail may be difficult to find at times and/or route-finding could be required. Off-trail hiking is also a possibility. Sections of a strenuous trail may be very exhausting and you can expect to find more than 2,000 feet of elevation gain on this category of trail.

TRAIL USE

Most trails in this book are suitable for three types of athletes: hikers, backpackers, or trail runners. In reality, the only difference between the three is that backpackers spend the night on the trail while the other two categories usually opt to return home. Backpackers prefer longer routes to justify camping outside whereas day hikers frequently opt for less distance. You will see all three categories of athlete on these trails, so be sure to smile and wave. After all, you are all out there enjoying Mother Nature.

PERMITS AND FEES

Various land management agencies utilize permits and fee structures, so you will see this vary from trail to trail. These fees and policies frequently change depending on the political climate and/or trail usage, so it is best to do research before leaving home. Call ahead to the local ranger station to be sure you don't show up to a trailhead empty-handed and permitless when a fee or permit is required.

And if you know permits are called for yet you don't have one? Be kind; do not bandit the trail. Sure, it is possible that you will not get caught, but permits are in place for a reason, and it is not because rangers enjoy policing our nation's trails. Permits frequently regulate the quantity of visitors to help preserve our trails, so follow the rules. This makes the wilderness a safer place for everyone.

Before You Hit the Trail

WEATHER & SEASONS

Weather is the great equalizer of hiking. It does not matter how fit you are or how much you enjoy the trail; poor weather can ruin a trip if you are unprepared. Plan ahead by doing your research from home. Watch the weather weeks in advance and as your trip draws closer, pay special attention to the weather patterns on your specific hike. Rainy weather is not always a reason to call off a trip, but communicate with others in your group. You may feel comfortable hiking through rain for three days but your partners may not. Additionally, consider your altitude and topographical location if you see nasty weather in the forecast. Rainstorms above tree line frequently bring lightning and thunder, both meteorological occurrences that can be deadly. Some hikes are prone to lightning strikes, so double-check the weekend forecast before hitting the dirt.

Trail seasonality is highly subjective. For example, the Shoup Bay Trail in Alaska is going to look much different than Georgia's Chattooga River Trail when January rolls around. Typically, summer is the best season for hiking in the west and at higher altitudes whereas southerners prefer winter or spring to escape the fiery hot and muggy conditions.

If you plan on hiking a high-altitude trail, keep the cooler temperatures in mind. In Colorado, for example, it could be 85 degrees and sunny at the trailhead but 55 degrees and sleeting a few thousand feet up. Additionally, snow lasts much longer as you climb higher in the mountains, so plan on encountering a few snowfields if you hike above tree line in early spring.

SAFETY, PREPARATION, AND GEAR

If there is only one piece of advice I can give you before your hike, it is this: Be Prepared! This is the motto of the Boy Scouts of America, and for good reason. If you plan accordingly and pack everything you need, there are very few instances where you will be caught in a bind.

The Ten Essentials

First and foremost, always pack the Ten Essentials. The Ten Essentials were a concept originally designed in the 1930s by the Mountaineers, a Seattle-based group of climbers and outdoor enthusiasts. In this original list, they included the ten items they felt any hiker would need to handle an emergency situation and safely spend a night or two outside. Since then, the original ten items have morphed into a systems-based list, but the ideology is the same. Theoretically, you will carry these systems with you on every hike, regardless of whether it is a multiday backpacking trip or a daylong hike. They are as follows:

1. *Navigation (map and compass):* Be sure to always bring a topographic map with you on any trip, as well as a compass. Pro tip: While it's great to have these items in your backpack, it is even more important that you know how to use them! Store the map in a ziplock bag or laminate it to ensure it doesn't get wet or destroyed. With modern technology, many hikers opt to carry GPS devices or even apps on their phone. While these are helpful and can be very useful, technology never replaces the tried-and-true map and compass. Gadgets break or quit or lose battery charge, but a map and compass will always work.

2. *Sun Protection (sunglasses and sunscreen):* A sunburn can ruin any trip, so always take the necessary precautions. Wear a hat to protect your face as well as sunglasses to cover your eyes. Never forget sunscreen and lip balm with SPF either.

3. *Insulation (extra clothing):* Be sure to always have an extra layer or two in case of emergency. Perhaps you take an accidental digger into a stream while hopping across some slippery rocks? You'll be psyched you brought extra clothing to keep you warm at camp.

4. *Illumination (headlamp or flashlight):* It's rare for a hiker or backpacker to bring a flashlight, but headlamps can be very useful. If your flashlight goes entirely sideways, it is always possible that you will conclude your hike in the dark. If this happens, a hands-free light will be absolutely critical. Also, cold weather can zap batteries, so make sure you bring an extra set with you on every trip.

5. *First-Aid Supplies:* Always, always bring medical supplies with you on every trip! And no, we're not simply talking about a box of adhesive bandages. Injuries happen on the trail and if your partner sprains her ankle while you are trekking 7 miles from the trailhead, you will be very thankful for the splint.

6. *Fire (matches or lighter):* Not only will some sort of flame be helpful when it comes time to cook dinner, but these tools are useful if you need to start an emergency fire. These days, most hikers opt for lighters over matches. Whichever you prefer, bring a backup in case your Plan A doesn't work out. Additionally, consider bringing a fire starter with you on every trip. These can be made at home (dryer lint or cotton balls smeared with petroleum jelly are popular choices) and weigh next to nothing, so there is no reason not to carry a few.

7. *Repair Kit and Tools:* Your dog will pop your sleeping pad one time while winter camping and you will learn your lesson (could have happened to anyone . . .). Make sure you pack the basic repair tools on every trip so you can fix any gear emergencies that crop up.

8. *Nutrition (extra food):* Always pack extra food, regardless of how long you will be on the trail. If you are planning on a simple day hike, bring an extra day's worth of calories. If you know you'll be out there for a few nights, plan on more extra food. Regardless of what you choose, be sure the food keeps over time and doesn't require cooking. After all, your emergency situation may mean a stove isn't available.

9. *Hydration (extra water):* Water is heavy (1 liter weighs roughly 2 pounds), but that doesn't mean you should skimp. Always pack extra to account for emergencies, and be sure to bring some type of filter or purification system so you can clean more if needed (and if a water source is available).

10. *Emergency Shelter:* No one wants to sleep in a blizzard during an unplanned night out, but these things occasionally happen. And if they do, you want to ensure you are as safe and protected as possible. Bring an emergency shelter like a small bivy, tarp, or reflective blanket. Each option weighs only a few ounces but provides copious amounts of mental support.

Be Bear Smart

Many of the hikes featured in this book run through bear country. After all, bears are everywhere! For the most part, these trails stay in black bear country, but brown bears (of which grizzlies are a subspecies) do live in states like Alaska and Idaho. It is a great idea to be prepared for either four-legged beast.

Brown Bear vs. Black Bear: What's the Difference?

Black bears are the gentle giants of the bear world and can be found in all but ten of the lower forty-eight states. While black bears may appear just as fierce and intimidating as a brown bear, it is better to think of them as playful cousins. They are much smaller than brown bears and are likely more concerned about finding your bag of food than finding you. Black bears are very smart and can climb trees, making them an annoying menace when it comes to food storage and caching. In fact, these bears are so intelligent that their problem-solving skills vetoed bear bags in favor of bear canisters in popular areas of California and New England; they decoded the bear bag!

Brown bears are scarier than black bears thanks to their aggressive personality. You can identify a brown bear by the hump on its back; black bears do not have one. While you certainly don't want to run into a brown bear while hiking, bears truly do not want anything to do with you and will usually only attack if provoked.

Food Storage in Bear Country

Keeping your food on lockdown is the best way to prevent bear interference with your trip. Many bear-heavy areas like Yosemite National Park require bear-resistant storage such as canisters or bear bags. If you opt for a bear bag, be sure you know and understand the guidelines for where to hang the bag and the appropriate distance from camp. Likewise, if you use a bear canister, be sure you know the guidelines for where to stash your canister overnight.

Moreover, always be cognizant of your camp kitchen while backpacking in bear country. Never, ever cook inside your tent as the wafting smell of food may linger on your equipment and invite an unwelcome guest inside during the night. Instead, keep your sleeping location, your camp kitchen, and your food storage location as three distinctly separate areas, creating a triangle of sorts. While this isn't foolproof, it's an effective method to spread out the smell of human food and minimize the likelihood of a bear entering camp while you are sleeping.

If you are day hiking, you still need to be aware of food storage. Believe it or not, bears have been known to gain access to locked vehicles parked at trailheads, all because they smelled a candy bar in the backseat. If you are hiking in bear country, be sure to transfer any and all food from your car to the food-storage lockers included in the parking lot.

LEAVE NO TRACE

Leave No Trace (LNT) is the de facto set of outdoor ethics to promote conservation and preservation in the backcountry, as well as minimize the human impact on our green spaces. The bedrock of this sustainability program is a list of seven guiding principles:

1. *Plan Ahead and Prepare:* Proper planning for any trip ensures you will leave as minimal an impact as possible. Know and understand high-usage times and avoid them. Research area-specific details so that you can better avoid causing further harm. For example, vegetation in high alpine zones takes 50–100 years to recover, so understanding this ahead of time may help you be more cautious in your actions.

2. *Travel and Camp on Durable Surface:* Good campsites are found, not made. Always try to pitch your tent on gravel, hard-packed dirt, rocks, or other sturdy surfaces as opposed to marsh or delicate grasses. Additionally, be sure to always

camp at least 200 feet away from lakes and streams to minimize your influence on the aquatic plant life and wildlife.

3. *Dispose of Waste Properly:* Many people dislike speaking about bathroom behavior but it's easily one of the most-discussed topics in the outdoors. We are all human, which means we certainly need to poop while on the trail. If this happens, no big deal, but follow the LNT-designed guidelines: Dig a cathole at least 6–8 inches deep and 200 feet away from water. Then, bury your poop in the hole, ensuring you properly cover it afterwards. And as for trash and litter? Pack it in, pack it out.

4. *Minimize Campfire Impacts:* As synonymous as fires have become with camping, they are rarely a good idea since they cause lasting impacts to the environment and especially damage vegetation that takes years to recover. If you are camping in a dispersed area with a designated fire ring, keep it small and use only small sticks that can be snapped by hand. Be sure the fire is out completely before leaving it unattended.

5. *Leave What You Find:* Remember in kindergarten when we all learned to look but not touch? That same principle applies to the wilderness. If you happen upon ancient artifacts or historic structures, check 'em out, but let them be without altering or taking them. Likewise, don't create new structures, build trenches, or otherwise change the experience. Think about what the area looked like when you arrived, and then aim to leave it the same *or better* for the next person.

6. *Respect Wildlife:* In recent years, the United States has seen an increase in human involvement with wildlife. Just because the mountain goats or deer come up to your campsite does not mean they are domestic; they are still wild animals. Never feed, follow, or approach these animals, and certainly try not to get too close. This is for both your safety and the animal's welfare.

7. *Be Considerate of Other Visitors:* We all hit the trail to gain a wilderness experience full of beauty and solitude. To that end, try your best to preserve that same experience for others. Don't blast your music while hiking or yell and shout late at night while camping close to others. Basically, mind your manners so everyone can equally enjoy their time outside.

Additionally, the twenty-first century has brought about a wave of new Leave No Trace discussions revolving around social media. Thanks to the power of platforms like Instagram and Facebook, millions of users are geotagging specific locations while showcasing stunning scenery. In turn, hundreds of thousands of new visitors are heading to that specific location to see the real-life version of what they enjoyed in the photo. As a result, heavily photographed locations are becoming overrun and abused.

Leave No Trace recently released a brief list of suggested social media guidelines for the digital era. They included the following tips:

1. *Tag Thoughtfully:* Avoid geotagging specific locations and instead tag the general area like "Rocky Mountain National Park." While this still encourages others to go outside, it protects the same locations from over-trafficking.

2. *Be Mindful of What Your Images Portray:* So frequently, popular social media influencers showcase photos of picturesque scenes with a colorful tent pitched below a towering peak. But there is one problem: that tent is pitched smack next to a body of water, and the account just subconsciously shared that with thousands of followers. Be aware of the images you share on your social media account to encourage your followers to conserve the wilderness just as you do.

3. *Give Back to Places You Love:* Get involved with volunteer projects to help give back to your favorite trails.

4. *Encourage and Inspire Leave No Trace in Your Social Media Posts:* Regardless of whether you have 100 followers or 100,000, encourage them to take care of green spaces too.

HIKING TIPS AND SUGGESTIONS

There are two ways to look at this. First, I could go off the rails and detail all of the necessary gear and equipment that will make your adventure more comfortable and easier. We could talk about backpacks and hiking shoes, tents and sleeping bags. Or, I could remind you of the old adage: Hike your own hike. But what does that really mean?

So frequently, I think newcomers to hiking get caught up in all of the details and fancy-sounding words. If you walk into any outdoor goods store, you will be bombarded with words like *denier* and *ultralight* and *shank* and *outsole*. And if you are already well versed in outdoor gear, that is great. These words are all important and make sense—once you are prepared to deal with them. But if they are as familiar to you as a foreign language, you are likely to feel overwhelmed. And I would hate for that to happen.

The spirit of this book lies with the women featured. Some of them are hardcore, robust athletes while others are outdoor inspirations who are passionate about wild spaces. Neither is right or wrong and you have to decide which trail works best for you. If you want to challenge yourself, check out the hikes detailed by Kalen Thorien, Shawnté Salabert, Sarah Herron, or Hilary Oliver. There is no shortage of burning lungs and heavy backpacks on those trails. Or, if you are just beginning and/or want a mellow day filled with just a touch of Mother Nature, take a look at the trails chosen by Shanti Hodges, Ambreen Tariq, or Rue Mapp. These women opted for these particular hikes especially for their inclusive nature and welcome attitude toward everyone, regardless of abilities.

So again, I say: Hike your own hike. That is up to you to decide.

PHOTOGRAPHY TIPS AND SUGGESTIONS

It does not matter whether you cart an elaborate camera with multiple lenses or a basic smartphone; you will certainly want to snap more than a few photos while on your hike. In doing so, you will accomplish the first requirement of great photography: getting out there. But once there, how can you ensure that you will shoot the best possible photos? Here are a few tips from Will Rochfort, the photographer who captured the image on the cover of this book.

1. *Always have your camera accessible.* If it is a hassle to find it inside your backpack, you are less likely to take the time to shoot photos. Instead, find a system that works for you. If using a smartphone, store it in your pants pocket or in the waist belt pocket on your backpack. If you are using a larger camera, come up with a carrying method. For smaller point-and-shoots, a small camera case looped through the sternum strap on your backpack works very well. For a larger DSLR camera, a front-carry pack provides the same accessibility while acting as a counterbalance to your backpack.

2. *Focus on the light.* Dramatic subjects can look boring in flat light while mediocre subjects can appear downright dazzling with a beautiful evening glow. Focus your photography on the best capture of the light. Often this means shooting in the early morning or evening; the least flattering light is the overhead sunshine of midday.

3. *Carry a tripod.* Yes, this is extra weight, but your photos will thank you! It doesn't need to be fancy; a light, compact tripod will work. Find an option that you are willing to carry since stabilizing your camera may be crucial to many of your desired photos.

4. *Don't forget the extras.* If you shoot with a DSLR, remember to pack all of the extra equipment like memory cards, batteries, a cloth to clean your lenses, polarizers, and a charger if needed. There is nothing worse than setting up a shot for a stunning backcountry sunset only to realize that your dead battery light is flashing.

5. *Pixels are cheap.* It is a digital era, which means we don't pay to develop every single photo anymore. Snap as many photos as you want; you can sort through and delete the unwanted captures once you return home.

6. *Always take the memory photos.* As a photographer, it is easy to get caught up in the "perfect" photos: a glorious sunrise, an action hiking shot, or a quick glimpse of the black bear as he wanders through the wildflowers. But don't forget to take those often-cheesy photos with your group smiling at camp or posing by the trailhead sign. They won't feel as glamorous as your other photos, but these are the ones that help preserve your cherished memories.

Map Legend

Municipal

≡⊂20⊃≡ Interstate Highway

≡⊂178⊃≡ US Highway

≡⊂107⊃≡ State Road

≡⊂263⊃≡ Local/County Road

==== Gravel Road

==== Unpaved Road

—··—·· Country Boundary

—··—· State Boundary

Trails

------ Featured Trail

------ Trail

Water Features

Body of Water

Marsh

River/Creek

Intermittent Stream

Waterfall

Spring

Symbols

≍ Bridge

▪ Building/Point of Interest

▲ Campground

🅿 Parking

≍ Pass

▲ Peak/Elevation

🎪 Picnic Area

🚻 Restroom

📷 Scenic View

○ Town

⑳ Trailhead

❓ Visitor/Information Center

Land Management

National Park/Forest

Wilderness Area

State/County Park

INGRID BACKSTROM

The Enchantments Trail
Leavenworth, Washington

It's not hyperbole to say that Ingrid Backstrom is a living legend. Born and raised in Seattle, Washington, Ingrid moved to Squaw Valley in 2000 to test the powdery slopes as a ski bum. She spent a few years entering freeskiing competitions, but it wasn't until everything fell apart that she saw success. After losing her passport and ultimately canceling a trip to Chamonix, Ingrid entered a local competition at the last minute, even going as far as borrowing money and catching a ride to get there. Fortuitously, the team for Matchstick Productions (a ski film production company) showed up at that same competition and watched her compete. They were so impressed with her skiing that they asked her to film with them, leading to 2004's film entitled *Yearbook*. The rest, as they say, is history. To date, she has appeared in nineteen ski films, been named *Powder*'s Female Skier of the

Ingrid Backstrom above Snow Lake JIM DELZER

Year five times, nabbed first ski descents in Greenland, Baffin Island, and China, and been awarded ESPN's Real Women 2013 People's Choice Winner.

The Enchantments Trail makes you work for it. This jewel of Washington's Alpine Lakes Wilderness is lush, green, and rugged with high mountain passes, slabs of protruding granite, and glistening lakes so sparkly that you'll think someone dumped fairy dust in the water. But paradise doesn't come without sweat equity; this trail is full of lung-busting climbs that will exhaust both your legs and your brain. Thankfully, you'll see quite a few mountain goats on the trail that will help take your mind off your sore quads.

Nearest Town: Leavenworth

Getting There: Head west on US 2 through Leavenworth before taking a left on Icicle Road. Drive roughly 8 miles on Icicle Road before taking another left turn onto Road 7601. Follow it past the first trailhead for roughly 3.5 miles until you see the Stuart Lake Trailhead.

Trailhead: Stuart Lake Trailhead **GPS:** N47 31.652', W120 49.249'

Fees and Permits: Permits are required for any overnight visits between May 15 and Oct 31. These permits are largely awarded in a lottery that takes place between Feb 15 and Mar 2 of each year. If any spaces are left after this, they will be allocated on a first come, first served basis via the https://recreation.gov reservation system. Day users only need to fill out a free day-use permit that is available at any trailhead accessing the Enchantments Permit Area.

Trail Users: Hikers, trail runners

Elevation Gain: 4,835 feet

Length: 18 miles (point-to-point)

Approximate Hiking Time: One long day or 1–3 days backpacking

Difficulty: Strenuous

Insider Info: Mountain goats are as prevalent as squirrels on this trail. While beautiful and fun to watch, be aware that they enjoy the salt that comes with human urine. It's not uncommon to turn around from a bathroom break and find a mountain goat directly behind you, so please use the privies whenever possible. Fall is a beautiful time to visit as the larch trees are in full color!

Managing Agency: Wenatchee River Ranger District

EXPERIENCING IT

Skiing is known to cause knee injuries but Ingrid seemed to be unstoppable. But her near decade-long streak came to an abrupt end in 2013 while on set filming for Sherpa Cinemas's new film. After skiing into the backcountry of Canada's British Columbia, she and the crew scouted a pillow line that appeared perfect for shooting. Named for their appearance, pillow lines are a ski term used when large boulders are covered in a heavy coating of snow, completely obstructing the actual rock. When in prime conditions, the fluffy snow sits elegantly atop the stones, visually imitating a cushy pillow. Skilled skiers can descend from pillow to pillow, plunging into the soft snow before launching and descending onto the next pillow.

Looking back toward Leavenworth from Prusik Pass INGRID BACKSTROM

Unfortunately, pillow lines can be a guessing game as even the most experienced of skiers can't always confidently predict what will be underneath the frozen layer of whiteness. Once Ingrid climbed to the top of the line, she noted that it looked flatter from above and questioned her route. But, ever the professional, she went for it. After all, it was a filming day! Things went well as she zipped down the line, catching pockets of air before launching to the next pillow, absorbing the impact with her knees like a seasoned pro. She crushed the line—until she hit the bottom pillow with a *thud*. The landing was harder and more hard-packed than expected, and Ingrid immediately felt pain in her knee.

Oh no.

Fast-forward a few months, and Ingrid was post-op for her ruptured patella tendon. As an athlete, she possessed nearly unshakeable confidence. After all, it was almost a prerequisite to accomplish the tasks required of her career. But rehab is notoriously emotionally taxing, burying both confidence and a sense of identity underneath the never-ending list of seemingly menial physical exercises. Six months of rehab loomed in front of her as dark and ominous as blackened storm clouds. Could she still challenge herself? Would her body be up to its usual physical tasks?

Personally, Ingrid was asking a big life question: Should she stay or should she go? After long-distance dating, Ingrid's boyfriend (and now husband) asked her to spend a summer with him in Leavenworth. Since Ingrid was still loving life in Tahoe, she was reticent to head north. Things were good in Tahoe and she didn't know that it needed to change. But then again, with months of rehab on the schedule, she figured now was

Goats guarding the top of Aasgard Pass with Dragontail Peak in the background
INGRID BACKSTROM

as good a time as ever. Why not explore the possibilities and shake things up a bit? A little change might be good for her.

It didn't take long for Ingrid to realize she had made the best choice for her, both personally and geographically. She quickly discovered the Enchantments, a verdant wonderland so packed full of jagged peaks and shimmering water that she believed

A LAND OF FAIRYTALES

In the late 1950s, Bill and Peg Stark made their inaugural voyage to the Enchantments. They fell so deeply in love with the area that they continued the tradition, returning every summer for the next 35 years and eventually moving to Leavenworth to start an outfitters business. During their numerous visits to the Enchantments, this beloved couple began naming various features with mythical endearments. In Lower Enchantments Basin, they dubbed larch trees, lakes, and jagged peaks with monikers such as Gnome Tarn, Naiad Lake, and Sprite. In the Upper Basin, they switched to Norse origins with nicknames like Lake Freya and Valhalla Cirque. Many locals still prefer to use the mythological nicknames, but the Starks were never able to convince the Forest Service. Instead, the standard names like Perfection and Isolation Lake appear on maps, but many prefer the romantic yet colloquial nomenclature created by the Starks.

Diving into Inspiration Lake to cool off
INGRID BACKSTROM

it to be from a fairy tale rather than her new neighborhood. Ingrid could scarcely believe her luck: How did this lush wilderness of contrasts exist in her new Cascadian backyard? She ached to explore this magical land of alpine lakes and granite peaks, but knew that pulling a permit was more difficult than recovering from knee surgery. So, she and her boyfriend decided on a major day: They would day hike the entire 18 miles.

With almost 5,000 feet of elevation gain, day hiking the Enchantments Trail is not an easy feat. Yet it is one frequently attempted thanks to the strict permitting system in place in the Alpine Wilderness. The draw is the almost ethereal beauty that is the Enchantments. Hikers can begin at either end—Stuart Lake Trailhead or Snow Lake Trailhead—and leave a car at the endpoint. It is more commonly hiked from Stuart Lake since that direction calls for 2,600 feet less of elevation gain over the entire route.

Hiking in the Enchantments area includes five different zones. The most popular for permits are the Snow Zone, Colchuck Zone, and the Core Enchantments Zone. The other two—Stuart Zone and Eightmile/Caroline Zone—see less action for permits. If hikers opt to begin their day at the Stuart Lake Trailhead as suggested, they would begin in the Stuart Zone and continue through the Colchuck Zone and the Core Enchantments Zone before concluding in the Snow Zone. For many, the Core Enchantments Zone is the highlight of an undoubtedly beautiful hike. Chock-full of aqua bodies of water

Descending to Inspiration Lake INGRID BACKSTROM

and shimmering white slabs of granite, the contrast in colors is similar to what can only be found in a box of crayons. Frisky mountain goats complete the scene, creating a wilderness utopia of sorts. But again, pulling a permit in the Core Enchantments section of the wilderness is akin to a golden ticket at Willy Wonka's Chocolate Factory; it doesn't happen that often.

Nineteen miles is a big day for anyone, but coming off surgery made the distance more challenging. Ingrid and her future husband tackled the day like she does anything else: with drive, determination, and copious amounts of confidence. They charged the climbs and held comfortable conversations on the downhills, all while marveling at the sparkling scenery surrounding them. Lake after lake magically appeared around every bend in the trail, almost like a hidden backcountry gem.

But the day wasn't easy and Ingrid will be the first to admit that. As the miles wore on and the unrelenting climbing continued, she broke down and cried. The physical demand of the trip was simply too much for her to handle and tears were the only release that felt good. But that is the thing about a good cry: once it is over, you can see the world more clearly, almost as if the release of moisture washes away all the negativity and leaves behind a healthy dose of perspective. In fact, it is these lower moments that truly highlight Ingrid's strength as one of the best female freeskiers in the world. She doesn't wallow in her misery or throw herself a pity party. Instead, she acknowledges those emotions, noting where and what they're doing, and then moves on. She allows logic to take the reins.

In the Enchantments, it was no different. After eating a snack, she allowed herself a few moments to sit on a rock and look around her, soaking in all of the unique intricacies Mother Nature displayed. She watched the leaves flutter in the breeze and listened to the wind waft through the upper air, as soft and sweet as a quiet whisper. She admired the alpine lakes glittering in the distance, wondering if fairies really did dump their excess glitter along the shoreline. She stared at the practically neon green carpet that covered the valley, enjoying how soft and lush it looked from miles away as it covered the natural world in mythological beauty.

She gave herself that moment to gain perspective. Once it passed, she was a new woman. She and her boyfriend finished the trek, tired and sore but oh so happy. She returned home eager to discover what was next on her docket, bolstered by her renewed sense of confidence from the Enchantments. Reinvigorated and full of spirit and enthusiasm, Ingrid couldn't wait to see what adventure she would find next.

THE HIKE

From the Stuart Lake Trailhead, follow the trail to the back side of Colchuck Lake. Cross through the boulders and skirt a sandy beach, continuing on as the trail begins to steeply climb over talus. This elevation gain is the start of Aasgard Pass (officially coined Colchuck Pass but more colloquially called Aasgard). The trail disappears, so follow the cairns as you climb (staying to the left of the larch grove about halfway up); as it steepens, it'll go from hands-and-feet scrambling back to larger boulders near the top. Now that you've arrived in the Upper Enchantments, hike through the rocks until dropping down to the plateau underneath Little Annapurna. The plateau ends as the trail continues east and down a steep hill to Inspiration Lake.

You'll continue on, dropping farther down as you hit Perfection Lake; this is the Middle Enchantments. Hike through meadows of grass along the eastern shore of the lake, eventually climbing up and around to Sprite Lake. Once you see McClellan Peak and Prusik Peak, you will know you have entered the Lower Enchantments.

The Enchantments Trail

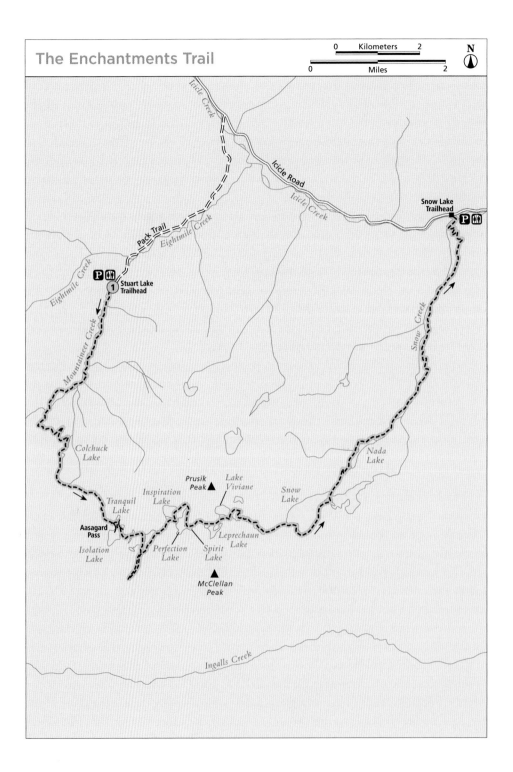

Descending between Leprechaun Lake and Lake Viviane INGRID BACKSTROM

Leprechaun Lake is the first body of water you see as you traverse along the shore before heading down to Lake Viviane. Continue hiking until you pass Nada Lake; this is the last of the lakes.

Cross the bridge and descend to the Snow Lakes Trail before following its steep path all the way back to the trailhead.

MILES AND DIRECTIONS

0.0 From the parking lot, begin on Stuart Lake Trail #1599.

1.5 Cross Mountaineer Creek on a log bridge.

2.25 Arrive at a trail junction. Stay to the left on Colchuck Lake Trail.

4.0 Reach the shores of Colchuck Lake.

4.5 Leave the south shore of Colchuck Lake to begin the initial climb up Aasgard Pass.

5.4 Stay to the left to continue up toward the summit.

5.6 Top out at the summit of Aasgard Pass.

7.0 Hit the shores of Perfection Lake, entering the Middle Enchantments.

7.4 Stay to the right, as the left is a detour up Prusik Pass.

10.1 Use a three-log bridge to cross Snow Creek.

11.2 Cross Snow Creek a second time via a crumbly dam.

13.8 Cross Snow Creek a third time.

16.5 Begin descending a series of steep switchbacks.

17.8 Cross Icicle Creek before reaching the end.

2

TERESA BAKER

Cataract Falls
Fairfax, California

Teresa Baker is a diversity advocate whose aim is to get more people outside so that it will endure for future generations. Based in California, she founded the African American Nature & Parks Experience (and subsequent African American National Park Event) in 2013 after a few visits to Yosemite National Park showed a decided lack of ethnic diversity. Her aim is to encourage more people of color to visit the parks

Teresa Baker, in her element VICTORIA REEDER PHOTOGRAPHY

while simultaneously encouraging the parks to hire more people of color. According to Teresa, this reciprocal relationship will benefit public land conservation and protection in the coming years when people of color comprise an even larger portion of the American population. Her efforts have created events such as the recreation of the Buffalo Soldiers Trail. In 1899, 1903, and 1904, over 400 African American soldiers journeyed from San Francisco's Presidio to protect the newly designated Yosemite and Sequoia National Parks as some of the first-ever park rangers. To commemorate this special group, Teresa organized a retracing of this route in 2013, with over 200 people attending the trek.

Located in the beloved Mount Tamalpais State Park, Cataract Falls is arguably the most popular waterfall in California's Marin County. While the number of people may not immediately place this hike on the top of your list, the serene nature of the cascading water, forest of wildflowers, and quietly murmuring trailside creek make it a perfect hike to help you get out of the city and into a peaceful meditative state before you can even say "Cataract."

Nearest Town: Fairfax

Getting There: From San Francisco, catch CA 101 N till it splits, then take CA 1 north toward Mill Valley/Stinson Beach. Drive on Shoreline Highway (CA 1 N) until the junction with Almonte. Turn left and drive roughly 2.5 miles until you hit the Panoramic Highway. Take a right, drive about 1 mile until you find the junction with Muir Woods Road, then stay straight to stay on the Panoramic Highway. After 4 more miles, take a right on Pantoll Road. Drive 1.5 miles before taking a left on West Ridgecrest Boulevard. Drive 3.7 miles before hitting the junction with Fairfax-Bolinas Road. Take a right, then drive roughly 2.2 miles until you see some small parking areas on the side of the road. Park here.

Trailhead: Roadside on Bolinas-Fairfax Road **GPS:** N37 56.220', W122 38.277'

Fees and Permits: Mount Tamalpais charges an $8 day use parking fee. This can be paid at the Pantoll Ranger Station or any of the designated pay stations.

Trail Users: Hikers, trail runners

Elevation Gain: 1,110 feet

Length: 2.7 miles RT (out-and-back)

Approximate Hiking Time: Half Day

Difficulty: Moderate

Insider Info: The trail is mostly shaded, which makes for a slippery walk in some places, especially on the many stairs. Bring trekking poles if you are prone to falling.

Managing Agency: Marin Municipal Water District

EXPERIENCING IT

She sat alone on the rock, pen and journal in hand, while watching the mesmerizing flow of water cascading in front of her as it bubbled through the various drops in the river before gurgling on to its next obstacle. Bigleaf Maple leaves glinted in the scattered sunshine, reflecting bits of light that permeated the thick forest canopy. Redwood trees stood proudly around her, strong and determined as they grew upward toward the clouds, reaching for bits of heaven far beyond what human eyes can see. Water levels were high thanks to a recent storm, so the foamy whitecaps thundered over the rocks, creating waterfalls so vivacious that it was difficult to delineate where the fall began and where it ended in the pool of crisp, cool water. Birds chirped a happy melody, reminding the world of their existence while hopping from branch to branch as they went about

It is easy to see where the nickname "Little Yosemite" comes from.
PAULINA DAO

their daily routine. The soothing warbles pierced Teresa Baker's thoughts as she leaned back against a rock, internalizing Mother Nature's welcome assault on her senses.

This was Cataract Falls.

Teresa enjoyed her moment of solitude on the rock, shocked that she seemingly had the entire place to herself. Why was the trail deserted? Why weren't more people

Cataract Falls Teresa Baker

enjoying this beautiful plot of wilderness just outside of the city?

But then again, not everyone enjoyed an outdoor childhood like Teresa. As the lone female in a sea of nine children, Teresa spent the greater part of her younger years outside, chasing after one of her many brothers at the family horse ranch. And when they came home, outdoor time didn't end. They lived across the street from a city park, offering prime access to long sunshine-filled days. Her mama kicked the kids out of the house every morning with direct instructions: "Don't come back until the street lights come on." That was all that Teresa and her brothers needed to hear. They spent their days creating various games to play, never knowing how each one would end but reveling in the creativity of imagination that reigns supreme in our earlier years. The world was their veritable playground and any day ending with grass-stained knees and mussed hair was considered a success.

Teresa's parents so strongly believed in an outdoor lifestyle that they continued to emphasize it with their choice of an after-school program. Teresa was just in grade school when her mother enrolled her and her two younger brothers in a program that, while educational, also emphasized outdoor playtime. The kids would spend their days indoors learning arithmetic and their afternoons expanding both their brains and their outdoor prowess.

It was a good childhood, and it directly shaped the woman Teresa is today. Sharp and bright eyed, there isn't much that escapes her notice. Her drive and determination are also noteworthy since she carries both traits like a shield of honor. Teresa is unique in the sense that she doesn't wait for assistance or clarification; she gets stuff done. This uncanny ability to hustle is arguably the motivating force behind the African American Nature & Parks Experience, and it likely stems from a rough and tumble childhood

A bridge along the Cataract Trail TERESA BAKER

with eight brothers. It could be easy to slip through the cracks or get steamrolled in a house full of boys, but Teresa doesn't operate like that. Because of this, it's more than fitting that it was also one of her brothers who first introduced her to Cataract Falls.

Her older brother called her up one day and asked if she wanted to go for a hike. Although it was close to home Teresa wasn't familiar with the trail, so she jumped at the chance to explore a new area. Any day outside was a good day as far as she was concerned, and truthfully, she didn't really care where they hiked. She just wanted to feel the soft earth beneath her feet and stretch her legs on a trail. She never suspected it would rival her tried and true favorite, Yosemite National Park, but that's exactly what happened.

MOUNT TAMALPAIS SCENIC RAILWAY

Mount Tamalpais State Park is a favorite for all of its outdoor recreational opportunities, but did you know a train used to be a big piece of the puzzle? After gold was discovered in the mid-1800s San Francisco's population boomed, and with the influx of people came a flood of locals interested in nearby Mount Tamalpais. Not only did they build some trails, they also created a wagon road to the top of the peak in 1884.

Eventually, the wagon road wasn't enough and the Mount Tamalpais Scenic Railway was built in 1896. Designed to carry visitors to the summit, some of the slopes were so steep that the railroad had to complete 281 curves in an effort to switchback its way up the hill, earning itself the moniker, "The Crookedest Railroad in the World." Additionally, a "gravity car" was created in 1907. Unlike the train, this car was designed to transport visitors from the top of the mountain into the depths of Muir Woods. This time, the railway used only gravity and a brake to control these open-air cars whose top speed was 12 mph. Guests loved the gravity cars and they remained popular until the advent of motor vehicles. Today, a recreation of a gravity car can be found in the Gravity Car Barn on East Peak.

A mini waterfall forms. PAULINA DAO

Cataract Falls is not an incredibly long hike, so it is telling that Teresa still managed to lose touch with her brother while hiking out. She fell farther and farther behind him as they climbed up the slippery steps of the trail, paying more attention to the insane beauty surrounding her than she did the actual hike. She couldn't believe her ethereal surroundings. Moss spread throughout the forest floor, spongy and damp with excess moisture gathered from one of the frequent storms. Mist hung in the air like a shroud, coating the horizon in a mystery cloak that offered just a bit of intrigue if you were willing to see through it. Teresa always hikes with a camera, so she pulled it out to snap so many photos that she finally quit stowing it, confident another stunning image would appear around the bend. She etched everything into memory: the glint of the water against the log bridge, the curve of the trees as they bent toward the falls, and the feel of the slick stone steps as her sneaker soles glided over them. Finally she sent her brother ahead, telling him she would find him later. She wanted peace and quiet to be alone with her thoughts as she mentally processed the overwhelming imagery she found zipping through her mind.

The steep stairs heading upward PAULINA DAO

This was the moment when Teresa sat down against the rock and pulled out her journal. Yosemite had long been her absolute favorite place on the planet for hiking, but she marveled at how small a world it must be to find a new favorite so close to home. If you catch it just right, like Teresa did, and witness Cataract Falls after a big rainstorm, the gushing water mimics what can be seen in the nearby national park, leading many to bestow the nickname "Little Yosemite" upon Cataract. Teresa marveled at the similarities and rejoiced that she had found a new outdoor paradise so close to home.

Over time, Cataract Falls has also become personal for Teresa. Sure, it was Yosemite where she first observed the lack of diversity that incited the creation of the African American Nature & Parks Experience, but that was not an experience unique to Yosemite. Cataract was similarly "whitewashed" when Teresa first hiked the trail. But as she returns various times over the years to enjoy her favorite trail during a welcome afternoon reprieve, Teresa notes improvement. People of color are hiking Cataract Falls and more individuals of varying demographics are finding their way

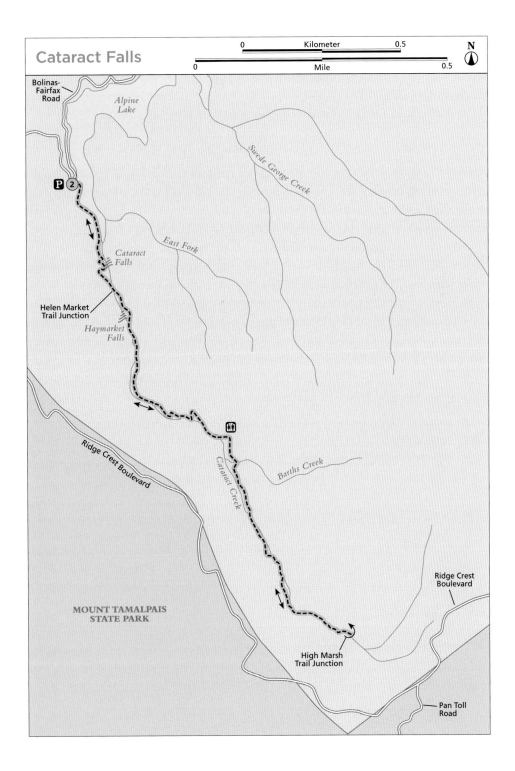

Cataract Falls

0   Kilometer   0.5

0   Mile   0.5

N

Bolinas-
Fairfax
Road

*Alpine
Lake*

Swede George Creek

P 2

East Fork

*Cataract
Falls*

Helen Market
Trail Junction

*Haymarket
Falls*

Cataract Creek

Barths Creek

Ridge Crest Boulevard

Ridge Crest
Boulevard

MOUNT TAMALPAIS
STATE PARK

High Marsh
Trail Junction

Pan Toll
Road

to her favorite place. She celebrates these changes. She enjoys sharing her trail with others, knowing that a larger outdoor community will mean more protection for these wild spaces later. These days, Cataract is a microcosm for what Teresa is hoping to accomplish on a larger level: the notion that nature is for everyone, and it doesn't take much work to seek it out.

For that reason, Teresa is elated to share her favorite place with the world.

THE HIKE

From the roadside parking, enter the forest on the trail. The trail quickly curves right as it runs along Alpine Lake; continue for roughly 300 feet before you see a fork. Stay to the right and begin gradually climbing upward. After crossing a bridge, you will encounter a set of stairs that are the first of many on this step-ridden hike.

Continue gradually hiking upward through the woods before the true climbing begins. Steeply hike through the switchbacks until you reach the bridge. Cross the bridge and find the junction with Helen Market Trail, then continue uphill to the right. After scrambling over a short but steep rocky section, the trail levels out. Continue upward through multiple sets of staircases before reaching the final set of falls and the junction with High Marsh Trail. Return the same way you came. ***Note:*** Many hikers prefer trekking poles as the staircases can be slick with moisture.

MILES AND DIRECTIONS

0.0 Begin at the roadside parking area on Bolinas-Fairfax Road.

0.1 Take a right.

0.5 Junction with Helen Market Trail; stay to the right.

1.3 Junction with High Marsh Trail; turnaround point.

2.6 Back at the roadside parking.

GINA BÉGIN

Gimli Ridge
Nelson, British Columbia

Gina Bégin is an adventure travel photojournalist and founder of Outdoor Women's Alliance, a volunteer-run nonprofit media and adventure collective designed to

Gina Bégin BRETT MALYSH

educate and empower women around the world. In 2017, Outdoor Women's Alliance (OWA) received one of twenty-six Force of Nature Fund grants from REI Co-op. With the $25,000 grant, OWA is funneling efforts into their Grassroots Program, nationwide social communities intended to connect women locally to create support systems and friendships via outdoor activities. With these funds, OWA is hoping to expand this particular program worldwide.

Currently, Gina acts as the executive director of OWA, the editor in chief for the OWA editorial mentorship program, and the director of their social media program. While born in Florida, she now resides in Nelson, British Columbia.

In Scandinavian mythology, Gimli is the equivalent to "heaven," making this an aptly named trail. Located in Valhalla Provincial Park, it is one of only two hikes in the Valhallas that reaches into the alpine area, but the epic views only come with serious sweat equity. This is a steep trail that gains almost 1,000 feet per mile, so be prepared for an arduous day. Wildlife is aplenty and you are sure to run into curious mountain goats and chattering marmots. As with most Canadian trails, be on the lookout for bears, as this is grizzly country.

Nearest Town: Nelson, British Columbia, Canada

Getting There: As with many hikes in this region, the approach isn't simple. From the Playmore Junction where Hwy. 6 departs Hwy. 3A, head north on Hwy. 6 for 28 miles. You will now be in Slocan. Turn left onto Gravel Pit Road. Once you do this, reset your odometer.

Drive across the Slocan River Bridge. When your odometer reaches 0.5 miles, stay left and continue on Slocan West Road. Cross over the Gwillim Creek bridge and then take a right on Little Slocan Road (1.4 miles). Drive along Little Slocan Road until you reach the junction at 8.1 miles, then turn right onto Bannock Burn Road. To keep things simple, reset your odometer here.

Start driving on Bannock Burn Road, but you will bear right very quickly (after roughly 100 yards). Drive another 200 yards, and then bear right a second time. Continue driving, staying straight at 5.2 miles. Eventually, you will curve right (6.5 miles) and drive up a steep uphill. Keep driving until mile 7.8, then bear left. The road very quickly (at 7.9 miles) curves sharply back, and you will reach the end of the road and Gimli Ridge Trailhead at 8 miles. ***Note:*** Due to budget cuts in British Columbia's provincial parks, this road has worsened. Clearance and a 4WD vehicle are recommended.

Trailhead: Bannock Burn Road **GPS:** N49 44.144', W117 38.653'

Fees and Permits: None

Trail Users: Hikers, backpackers, trail runners

Elevation Gain: 2,510 feet

Length: 5.92 miles RT (out-and-back)

Approximate Hiking Time: One Full Day

Difficulty: Strenuous

Insider Info: Thoughtful park rangers leave chicken wire in the parking lot for hikers to wrap around the base of their vehicles. Marmots and mice are aplenty, and they will chew through vehicle wiring and anything else they can get their teeth on, so it is highly recommended that you use it.

Managing Agency: Valhalla Provincial Park

EXPERIENCING IT

Gina Bégin will be the first to admit it: She didn't like hiking.

There was something about the perceived monotony of placing one foot in front of another, slowly plodding along while hefting a typically heavy load on your shoulders, feeling the weight of the pack compressing your spine as your heart pounded and lungs burned. In fact, it is easy to understand: Hiking is not comfortable.

Many might find this odd. After all, Gina is the founder of Outdoor Women's Alliance (OWA), one of the first nonprofits dedicated to female empowerment and

---

NORSE MYTHOLOGY IN THE VALHALLAS

With their stunning beauty, it seems only logical that the features in the West Kootenay are largely named after famous Norse mythological figures. In fact, Valhalla itself is taken from Scandinavian folklore. Valhalla was a majestic and gigantic hall that the god Odin presided over. Led by Valkyries, half of those soldiers who died in combat were chosen by Odin to travel to Valhalla (while the other half went to Fólkvangr, Freyja's field).

In addition to Valhalla, numerous names in this area carry Norse origins. Asgard Peak, Gimli Peak, the Valkyr Range, Mt. Odin, Mt. Freya, and Hoder Creek are all examples of names from Scandinavian lore used in this Canadian range.

First sight of a few peaks in the Valhalla Range GINA BÉGIN

companionship in the outdoors. While hiking isn't a requisite for participation, it is arguably one of the more common activities scheduled on OWA's local grass-roots calendars. Groups of women from Colorado to Canada and Washington to New England embark upon group hikes as a means of finding female camaraderie mixed with a touch of self-confidence.

While Gina never enjoyed hiking, she surely understood its powers. As a child growing up in the northern portion of Florida, Gina and her twin brother enjoyed playing in the backyard forest that was central to their universe. But when she was 8 years old, her single mother received a teaching job offer that whisked the family away to the other side of the country. They left behind the ocean and swampland for the canyon country and foothills of southern Utah. It was a small town of 1,800 people and Gina's family was even more removed, living just outside of the town center. Her mother worked during the day and attended school at night, enduring a round-trip commute of 4 hours every day. Gina and her brother enjoyed plenty of freedom. After they finished their chores and ate dinner, they had free rein of the foothills behind their house. With minimal adult supervision and a swath of mountains at their disposal, they explored every inch of the hillsides. They learned about hiking and camping and skiing, all activities that were new to them after a more structured outdoor experience in Florida. Gina also learned a lot about self-reliance and independence, characteristics

The locally iconic Gimli as it first comes into view on the trail GINA BÉGIN

that are intrinsic to outdoor experiences, especially if you are making decisions for yourself.

The family eventually returned to Florida, only this time they ended up in the southern portion, where retirees were more common than kids. Gina observed that towns were focused on catering to the snowbirds that fled south when the northern weather turned cold. As a result, the community frequently overlooked the youth and many of Gina's friends turned to bad behavior and gangs. Girls dropped out of school with teenage pregnancies. Dads ended up in jail facing murder charges. Friends ended up hooked on the drugs and violence that accompanied the gang behavior.

Gina tries to keep her distance as the (locally) infamously friendly family of mountain goats follows her down the trail.
Brett Malysh

While many of her close friends succumbed to these pitfalls, Gina managed to keep it together, something she still credits to her outdoor experiences in Utah. Exploring the foothills behind their home had provided her with the skill set needed to make good choices and understand the consequences of her actions. She had confidence in herself and believed in her abilities; these traits stemmed directly from her solo explorations out west. They worked in her favor as she continued through high school, watching as various friends and acquaintances struggled, eventually capitulating to a wayward lifestyle.

Upon graduation Gina left, not wanting to be shackled to the urban environment, rife with unwise choices. She ventured west, returning to the place where she first fell in love with the wilderness: Utah.

She attended university and took outdoor courses, earning certifications in ski instruction and avalanche awareness. As she grew more involved in these outdoor experiences, she felt the urban pressure fall away, almost as if a weight had been released from her shoulders. It was then that the kernel of the idea for OWA came to her. If the rejuvenating power of the outdoors had helped her so much, imagine what it could do for women all over the country!

Years passed and Gina continued to grow OWA as she moved about the country. She lived in her car for a year while driving throughout North America in search of outdoor stories and pristine adventures. She eventually found love—and a forever home—in Nelson, a thriving community in the Selkirks of British Columbia with enviable ski terrain and breathtakingly scenic hikes out her front door. But still, Gina couldn't latch on to hiking and if anything, grew less interested in the hobby. It made

Gimli and the surrounding alpine meadow GINA BÉGIN

her uncomfortably hot—something she willingly left behind in Florida—and the mystery of British Columbia's hiking trails left her frustrated, with their dense trees that shrouded views and hid obstacles that existed just around the corner. She understood others enjoyed these arduous adventures and certainly recommended trekking for her friends, but as for her? No, thank you. She would stick to skiing and mountain biking.

But then, as if by divine interference, her perspective changed in a single day.

While shuttling her mountain biking enthusiast boyfriend to a trailhead one day, she rumbled around the bend of a small dirt road and stopped the car in its tracks. The thick forest opened up into a clearing and before her lay the most magnificent slab of granite she had ever seen. The sheer face was warmed by the sun, almost as if heaven had opened up in an effort to highlight this stupendous massif for her eyes only. This was Mt. Gimli.

Immediately, Gina knew she needed to explore the area. She convinced her boyfriend to play tour guide and planned a trip to Gimli Ridge. She had once seen the Valhallas in a ski film, impressed by their grandeur but completely unaware of where they were or how she would ever get there. Seeing them appear in front of her almost seemed like a sign; she was meant to hike this trail.

The weekend approached and Gina and her boyfriend endured the seemingly never-ending approach to the trailhead, complete with a downed tree that threatened to thwart their plans before they even got started. But then they arrived, and Gimli was everything she had dreamt of a hiking trail—and more.

To be sure, the voyage upward was steep, and certainly steeper than Gina preferred while hiking. She huffed and puffed, her quads incessantly screaming as she trailed behind her boyfriend. For the first time in forever, she didn't hate the hike. She

The view from the ridge into Mulvey Basin, including Mulvey Lakes BRETT MALYSH

enjoyed the mystery as she rounded each bend, eager to experience whatever beauty this trail had in store. She crept up to the saddle to find her boyfriend quietly sitting on a rock, watching her with an unassuming look on his face. She briefly considered heckling him for crushing the impossibly steep climb, but she was distracted once she saw the view. In front of her lay the imposing Mt. Gimli, its steep spire soaring to the sky while specks of granite shimmered in the sunlight. A family of mountain goats wandered by, absolutely unaware of how their exquisite home was affecting Gina.

It was a moment she clearly remembers. Overwhelmed by the beauty around her, Gina didn't know what to do other than sit down on a rock, make herself comfortable, and quietly soak in her surroundings. She observed the goats and marveled at Mt. Gimli. She watched the yellow sun rays stream down as dust particles danced in and out of their warmth. She wondered at the color of the alpine lake below, questioning whether Mother Nature had simply melted a box of crayons in the water.

She does not know how long she sat on the rock, admiring the natural world, but it certainly changed her. Trekking to Gimli Ridge changed her perspective about hiking.

A section of the hike that moves past
Gimli and to the ridge GINA BÉGIN

She still isn't sold on hiking in general, but if you ask her to hike to Gimli Ridge? She will join you every time.

THE HIKE

Once you exit your vehicle, you will see Gimli Peak looming in front of you. Don't let your eyes deceive you: The commanding peak is not as close as it appears and you still have some formidable climbing ahead of you for the day!

From the trailhead, your route immediately begins climbing through brushy clear-cut growing toward the trail, creating a tight, scratchy singletrack. After 10 minutes of movement, you cross over a small stream via a bridge and trade the brush for a densely wooded forest. Continue hiking up as the unrelenting terrain climbs through steep switchbacks. Until you hit the alpine, this route is technically very easy and won't require anything other than placing one foot in front of the other. By Canadian standards, this makes this hike "easy," but don't be fooled. You will gain nearly 1,000 feet in elevation for every mile you hike, so this is a steep trek.

After one mile of climbing, the trees thin and you enter the alpine. From here, the trail fades as it curves north–northwest as you ascend to the shoulder. Hike for roughly 30–45 minutes across the grassy and rocky hillside, eventually catching a glimpse of the uniquely shaped Mt. Gimli. You will know you have reached the shoulder when you see a small windbreak constructed from loose pieces of shale. Some hikers opt to camp here; it can also be used as a food cache. There is a composting toilet here.

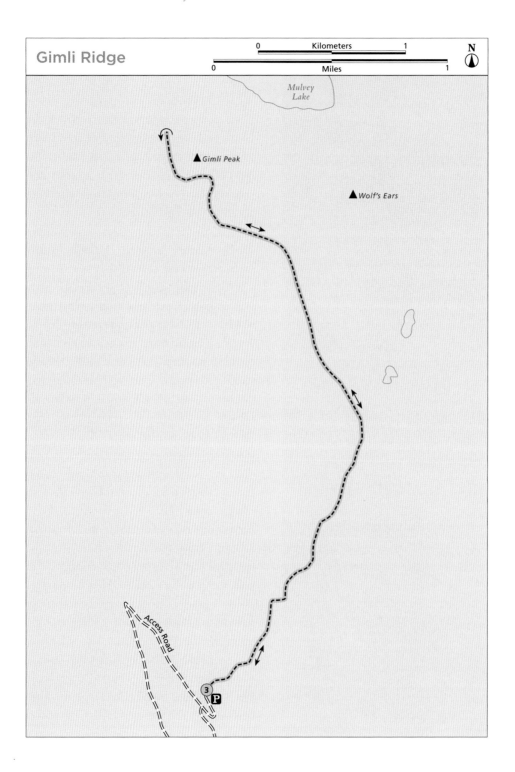

Gimli Ridge

0   Kilometers   1

0   Miles   1

N

Mulvey Lake

▲ *Gimli Peak*

▲ *Wolf's Ears*

Access Road

3
P

View of Mulvey Basin and Mulvey Lakes with a snowfield GINA BÉGIN

As you look toward Gimli Peak, you will see a small saddle to the west. This is Gimli Ridge. A small track can also be seen winding along the base of the peak, eventually connecting with the ridge. Take this small trail for roughly 45 minutes and you will find yourself on Gimli Ridge, with commanding views of Mulvey Basin and Asgard Peak. Some scrambling is required. ***Note:*** Some hikers opt to spend the night on the ridge and return to the trailhead the following day. Others continue on to summit Mt. Gimli itself. There is a small campsite on the ridge, as well as another food cache and composting toilet.

MILES AND DIRECTIONS

0.0 Begin at the end of the access road where you parked your car. Look for the sign that indicates Valhalla Provincial Park.

0.2 Cross a small stream via the bridge.

0.4 Trail junction; stay straight and continue climbing.

0.9 You've reached tree line; continue hiking into the alpine.

1.4 The trail flattens out temporarily and affords you a breather.

2.5 You've reached the first windbreak and a small toilet on the saddle.

3.0 You've reached the base of Gimli Peak. Unless you are spending the night or tackling the peak itself, turn around and retrace your steps back to the trailhead.

KATIE BOUÉ

Bonneville Shoreline Trail
Salt Lake City, Utah

Katie Boué is a Cuban-American outdoor advocate with two rules in life: Be a decent human and do good. A Miami native, she ventured west and fell in love with the desert sunsets, red sand, and wide open spaces of Utah's canyon country. After first settling in

Katie Boué Jo Savage

Denver and then finding her home in Salt Lake City, she forged a career for herself via the powers of social media. Through platforms such as Instagram, Katie has become a loud and proud voice in the outdoor industry who expounds on the protection and conservation of our public lands. She is also a social media freelancer and writer whose natural ability to organically amplify a brand's message has made her a sought-after strategist in the outdoor arena. In her spare time, she loves trail running, rock climbing, and riding her bike to the local farmer's market with her dog, Spaghetti.

Not all hiking trails begin or end in the middle of nowhere wilderness. In fact, many favorite hikes are revered for their simplicity and ease of access. Salt Lake City's Bonneville Shoreline Trail is one such path, and is a local favorite thanks to its appeal to the masses. The trail is passable all year long, even in the winter when its frequent users typically pack down a route before the sun rises. With various trailheads scattered throughout the city, outdoor enthusiasts can easily find a trailhead that works for them.

Nearest Town: Salt Lake City

Getting There: From South Temple Street, head north on B Street. At the intersection of B Street and 11th Avenue, continue on Bonneville Boulevard as it descends into City Creek Canyon. Stay on the right of the one-way street. You may park in the small pullout on the right side of the road at the bottom of the canyon or in the main parking lot just beyond the City Creek gate.

Trailhead: City Creek Trailhead **GPS:** N40 47.400', W111 52.766'

Fees and Permits: None

Trail Users: Hikers, trail runners, mountain bikers

Elevation Gain: 1,110 feet (for this section)

Length: 8.8 miles RT (out-and-back)

Approximate Hiking Time: Full Day

Difficulty: Easy–Moderate

Seasonal Highlights: There is minimal tree coverage, which makes for some warm summer days but also means it is an easy trail to visit in spring because it dries out quickly.

Managing Agency: Bonneville Shoreline Trail Coalition

Hiking one of the BST's many offshoot trails BRODY LEVEN

EXPERIENCING IT

On a Tuesday in early October, Katie Boué drove into Salt Lake City with tears of contentment streaming down her cheeks. The familiar skyline crept into view as the Wasatch Range soared toward the heavens as if reaching for the sun itself.

Days later, she awoke to one of those crisp fall mornings when the arid breeze crackles as it whips through your hair, blowing it back and forth as if waving goodbye to the warm summer days. A Florida native, Katie's oxygen-deprived lungs burned in the high-altitude air and infamous inversion as she laced up her running shoes and set out to explore her new home.

Her leg muscles stretched like dry rubber bands, yearning for both elasticity and movement that was tough to find after months in a car. As if they had a mind of their own, her sneakers carried her through the University of Utah campus, steadily pounding against the solid concrete of the city's sidewalks. Her blood coursed in her veins and her cheeks flushed with anticipation as she crossed a parking lot glistening with frost. Her feet met the soft earth of the trail and a big beautiful sign welcomed Katie to the Wasatch National Forest.

This was the Bonneville Shoreline Trail. And for Katie, this trail was synonymous with home.

Months previously, Katie purchased those very same running shoes during one of her numerous stopovers in Salt Lake. You see, life on the road can be both lonely and exhilarating, a fact that Katie discovered firsthand. As an outdoor advocate and social media strategist working for the Outdoor Industry Association (OIA), Katie successfully pitched what many would call a dream job: a 4-month solo road trip dubbed the OIA Roadshow. From June–September of 2016, Katie crisscrossed the country while living in her adorable yet compact cargo van. She covered 10,000 miles in nine different states while conducting meetings with various OIA members in an effort to establish on the ground relationships.

And she got to do it while exploring the American West from her newly minted mobile home of sorts.

It was the definition of hipster freedom. No cubicle! No bumper-to-bumper commute! No inane conversations in the break room! But Katie wanted more. She wanted a home, a place to store her quick draws and climbing ropes, a tree from which to hang twinkly lights at Christmas, and a local farmers market to call her own.

In a way, the Roadshow was an experimental platform that helped establish the next evolution of her identity. As a late-20s single gal, Katie had swapped through multiple versions of herself: College graduate, copy writer, rock climber, van lifer, girlfriend, and social media influencer were merely a few monikers she carried. But all of them fit like that trusty sweater hiding in the back of your closet—it suits you, but is it really what you want to wear for the rest of your life?

The blend of the city and the mountains is one of the most appealing aspects of the BST. KATIE BOUÉ

Was finding yourself as simple as trying on a new sweater? Could she discover her ideals, her principles, and her future on the road to her next OIA client meeting?

Those 4 months were a period of deep introspection as she turned her pint-sized cargo van into a home on wheels. Her routine was enviable by outdoor dirt bag standards. She slept in the back, affording her the freedom to camp out under the stars at any big-sky locale of her choosing. She typed online content while sipping lattes at bustling coffee shops dotted across the western United States. Her job required numerous conference calls where visibility wasn't a factor. As long as she had cell service, it didn't matter whether she was at the crag or hefting a backpack to her next campsite. Katie hiked and climbed wherever and whenever she wanted as long as it didn't interfere with her work.

She also began running. And it was during one of her many Salt Lake layovers that she stumbled upon the Bonneville Shoreline Trail (BST).

The existing BST stretches for just over 100 miles (plus numerous connectors and unofficial spur trails) along the shoreline of the ancient Lake Bonneville, the precursor to the Great Salt Lake. This prehistoric pluvial lake once covered over 19,000 square miles, or over half of Utah. At its prime, the lake reached as far west as Nevada, north into Idaho, and into southern Utah. However, the lake dramatically receded after the Bonneville Flood 15,000 years ago. Climate change then took its toll, causing the remainder of the lake to dry up and leave behind small remnants in the form of the Great Salt Lake, Utah Lake, Sevier Lake, Rush Lake, and Little Salt Lake. What we are left with today is a geological feature known as the Bonneville Shelf.

Early winter snow blanketing BST stretches near the University of Utah Jo SAVAGE

These days, you're unlikely to see any woolly mammoths cruising along the BST but you will run into quite a few hikers, walkers, runners, and bikers. The existing mixed-use trail undulates across the Wasatch Front, including Salt Lake City. The core trail sees a fair amount of traffic, which means the snow is always packed during the winter months. Thanks to the lack of tree cover, it's dry and dusty in the summer but usually one of the first trails to become usable in the spring.

Accessibility is the name of the game with the BST. Currently, three main parking areas exist in Salt Lake City proper, with dozens more scattered across the existing 100 miles. Salt Lake locals can easily log miles post-work and pre-happy hour on a Friday evening. And the accessibility is increasing in the future, with plans to extend

Trail running along the BST near City Creek Jo SAVAGE

THE BONNEVILLE FLOOD

These days, it's a mysterious horizontal line stretching along the Wasatch Range. The line is continuous, constant, and steady as it wraps around every rock outcropping, every inland surge of land, and every geographic feature as far as the eye can see. This enigma can be seen around much of Utah and is so distinct that it's easy to spot from a distance.

This puzzling line indicates the former shoreline of the massive inland lake known as Lake Bonneville. The sprawling behemoth covered a majority of Utah, making the present-day Great Salt Lake look like a tiny fishing pond. Imagining such a gargantuan body of inland water can be difficult, but what is more fascinating is envisioning the flood that caused the water levels to drop so dramatically.

Climate changed abruptly during the Pleistocene Epoch, and this rapid warming caused glaciers to quickly melt. Even a body of water the size of Lake Bonneville couldn't hold the enormous influx of glacial runoff, so it overfilled thanks to the massive contribution from the Bear River. With this surplus, a new body of water broke through Red Rock Pass in southeastern Idaho, beginning what we now refer to as the Bonneville Flood. The thunderous deluge gushed westward through the Pocatello Valley and up through the Marsh Valley before flowing along the Snake River Plain.

The effect of the Bonneville Flood is telling of its parent lake's size. According to scientists, the peak release from Red Rock Pass lasted for over 8 weeks and lowered Lake Bonneville by over 350 feet. It accounted for a loss of almost 3,000 cubic miles of water. *That's a lot of water!* But more pertinently, this flood began the downsizing of Lake Bonneville, a process that continued for thousands of years until it settled into today's Great Salt Lake. Users of the Bonneville Shoreline Trail can thank this flood for freeing up the land they now so spiritedly enjoy.

the trail even farther. As it currently stands, BST efforts will hopefully grow the trail until it begins at the Idaho border north of Logan before winding more than 280 miles south toward its subsequent terminus in Nephi.

However, the banner characteristic of the BST is truly its versatility. Everyone is welcome on this citywide favorite. The trail rolls—rather than dramatically leaps—into the foothills, making it a quality option for beginners and advanced athletes alike. In fact, it's not uncommon to see a runner completing his first mile alongside a seasoned ultra-marathoner. That's the beauty of the BST. It's a nonpareil example of close to home recreation, and in a way is an iconic representation Salt Lake's outdoor community.

By late summer, the heat has taken its toll and the grass and shrubbery turn dry and crunchy. KATIE BOUÉ

At least, that was how Katie felt the first time she clapped eyes on this portion of earthly dirt.

As her OIA Roadshow wound to a close, Katie found herself continually drawn to both Salt Lake and the BST. Her feelings about the trail itself could be considered a microcosm of the city as a whole. The BST is inclusive, welcoming, and offers a little bit of everything for anyone who wishes to explore it; this is precisely how Katie felt about Salt Lake City.

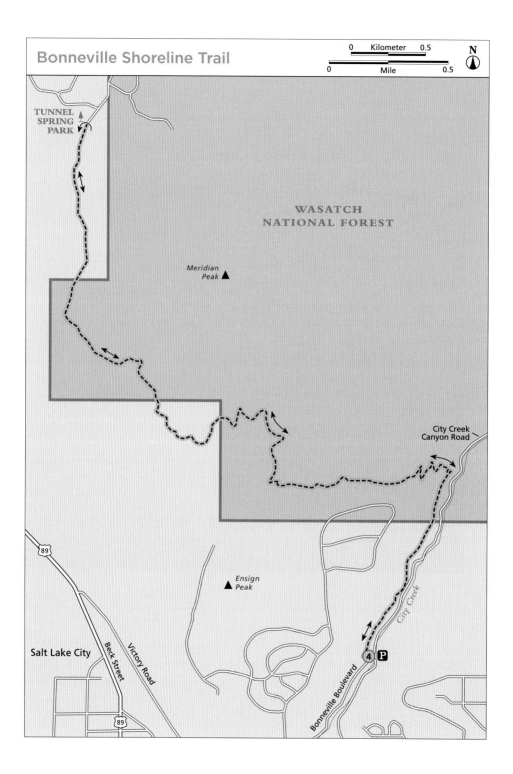

Bonneville Shoreline Trail

0   Kilometer   0.5

0   Mile   0.5

N

TUNNEL
SPRING
PARK

WASATCH
NATIONAL FOREST

*Meridian
Peak* ▲

City Creek
Canyon Road

*Ensign
Peak* ▲

89

City Creek

Salt Lake City

Beck Street

Victory Road

4 P

Bonneville Boulevard

89

Katie returned to Salt Lake City dozens of times before permanently moving there, and each time she was drawn back to the BST. As someone who previously abhorred even the thought of running and considered hiking to be a necessary evil required to arrive at the local crag, the BST inspired a new awakening within her. Her warm-blooded preferences faded as she experienced her first-ever cold weather runs along the trail, progressing from frozen dirt to slush and eventually to knee-deep snow on one of the many mountainous offshoots.

The BST remained steadfast throughout the changing of the seasons and Katie continued to explore her new favorite haunt. Over time, her legs grew in confidence and her lungs developed increased stamina. She settled into her new hometown and established a career that she is passionate about: outdoor advocacy. Everything came full circle, beginning and ending with the Bonneville Shoreline Trail.

THE HIKE

From the trailhead, you'll immediately begin gently climbing north, following the steeplechase training course. The trail then turns left, steeply climbing switchbacks for roughly ½ mile before leveling out again. It grows steeper once more around the second mile marker, affording hikers spectacular views of the city, especially at sunset. The rollers continue with the trail eventually turning west. You will eventually merge with a dirt road before pushing up the final bit of climbing to a set of radio towers.

From the radio towers, the descent begins. It's rocky near the top but gradually gives way to loose dirt as you continue hiking through open meadows. There is one last small uphill before the trail descends and eventually flattens out as it coasts into Tunnel Springs Park. From here, turn around and retrace your steps back to your car.

MILES AND DIRECTIONS

0.0 From the parking area, walk across Bonneville Boulevard and pick up the trail on the other side of the road.

1.0 Take a left and begin hiking up the switchbacks.

1.3 Keep ascending through the series of rollers.

2.1 Great view of sunset over the city.

3.0 Trail merges with a dirt road.

3.2 You've reached the radio towers; stay straight to maintain the Bonneville Shoreline Trail.

3.7 Trail intersection; stay straight.

4.15 The trail forks; stay to the left.

4.4 You've reached Tunnel Spring Park. Turn around to return to your car.

JAINEE DIAL & LINDSEY ELLIOTT
Pamelia Lake to Hanks Lake
Detroit, Oregon

Jainee Dial and Lindsey Elliott are the cofounders of Wylder Goods, the first online outdoor gear retailer solely for women. Based in Utah, this benefit corporation launched in 2016 after hosting a successful Kickstarter campaign. Initially, the goal was personal: Neither woman could find outdoor gear they liked. But as they

The cofounders of Wylder Goods: Lindsey Elliott (left) and Jainee Dial JORDAN PAY

continued working on their project, Wylder Goods evolved. Now, the retailer wants to change the narrative about women in the outdoor industry while continuing the discussion around gender. Sustainability is also important to the Wylder team and they expect their brand partners to utilize an ethical supply chain. You can visit them online at WylderGoods.com.

This is arguably one of the most popular hiking destinations in the Mt. Jefferson Wilderness, and for good reason. Stunning wildflower blooms, lushly carpeted forests, cascading falls, and glistening freshwater lakes are just a few of the reasons locals and tourists alike enjoy this corner of the globe. The first half of the trail to Pamelia Lake can be crowded with day hikers, but the people thin as you pass Pamelia and head toward Hanks Lake. Enjoy the solitude!

Nearest Town: Detroit, Oregon

Getting There: From the Detroit Ranger Station in Detroit, travel east on OR 22 for roughly 14 miles. Turn left onto Pamelia Creek Road (Forest Road 2246). Drive for 5 miles until you reach the end of the road. Parking will be on the left side and fits 20 vehicles.

Trailhead: Pamelia Lake Trailhead **GPS:** N44 39.601', W121 53.492'

Fees and Permits: A recreational pass for your car is required for $5. Additionally, you also need limited entry permits for both day and overnight use visits to Pamelia Lake and the Hunts Cove area near Hanks Lake. This is a $6 per vehicle per day fee. If you reserve in advance, there is an additional $10 nonrefundable processing fee. To reserve, visit recreation.gov.

Trail Users: Hikers, backpackers, trail runners

Elevation Gain: 2,169 feet

Length: 10.6 miles RT (out-and-back)

Approximate Hiking Time: Two Days

Difficulty: Moderate–Strenuous

Insider Info: Beware: Occasional algae blooms occur at Pamelia Lake. These rapid increases in freshwater algae in the water can injure animals and the ecology, so it is best to stay out of the water when such an event occurs (and never use it for drinking water!) The rangers always leave signage at the trailhead, so keep your eyes peeled for notices.

Managing Agency: Willamette National Forest

EXPERIENCING IT

Every entrepreneur has that single experience that sparks a lightbulb in the recesses of their mind. For Lindsey Elliott, all it took was 28 days of chilly, wet darkness to inspire Wylder Goods.

While working in the nonprofit sector, Lindsey received a call from Gina Peters, now brand partnerships director of Wylder, inviting her on a decidedly Type II fun experience: a month-long winter rafting trip in the Grand Canyon. There were very few people who could handle 28 days of minimal sunshine and frigid water, but Gina knew Lindsey was up to the task.

The timing was impeccable as Lindsey was at a crossroads in her life. She would soon be leaving the nonprofit sector to return to graduate school and was juggling a few other career options. Having recently moved in with Jainee Dial, Lindsey certainly already had Wylder Goods floating around in the muddled web of her brain. But it was merely a seed of ideation while her other options were more concrete and potentially realistic. Perhaps it was the lack of quality women's gear while on the trip. Or maybe Lindsey only needed 28 days of unadulterated contemplation without the interference of life's inherent chaos. Whatever the reason, she returned from the Grand Canyon ready, able, and willing to devote herself to Wylder.

The Wylder women remember it clearly. It was March 2015, and the two sat on the couch in the living room of their shared Northern California home, sipping whiskey and cozying up to the warmth of the woodstove. Ever since selling her travel company Nomad, Jainee had ruminated on the idea of a female-based digital marketplace. She was as eager as Lindsey to take the outdoor industry by storm. They hashed out the details of their plan, poured another glass of whiskey, and jumped into the proverbial deep end.

Jainee and Lindsey know how to hustle, which is evident in the evolution of Wylder Goods. It took them just over one year to carry the concept from the ideation stage to the funding stage via a Kickstarter campaign they launched in April 2016. Kickstarter was quite common, but it was rare to fundraise based on a concept rather than a product. Nevertheless, the women had struck a nerve with their core audience. They raised close to $55,000 in 30 days—almost $10,000 over their initial goal.

As is standard with Kickstarter campaigns, Wylder offered various prizes to donors. For the 6 backers that pledged $500, Jainee and Lindsey proffered a unique and Wylder-appropriate reward: a guided backpacking trip with the women of Wylder.

The Wylder Duo MARCUS MACDONALD

Months passed and the warm days gradually slipped into the brisk mornings of early fall. Wylder Goods was approaching their official go-live date in November and Jainee and Lindsey were busy fulfilling the rewards promised by the campaign. In particular, the women prepared for the upcoming backpacking trip to the Mount Jefferson Wilderness Area in the Cascade Range of Oregon. The women who supported their campaign with such large donations were critical in Wylder surpassing their fundraising goal, so Jainee and Lindsey wanted to ensure they felt appreciated in return.

Hitting the trail towards Pamelia Lake WYLDER GOODS

Choosing a trail was easy: They would tackle the 11-mile trek to Hanks Lake via Pamelia Lake. Almost like a real-life Fern Gully, this hike is filled with lush green foliage that reaches out trailside to whisper against the arms of hikers as they walk on to their next destination. The Pacific Northwest highlights soft terrain with babbling creeks and splashing waterfalls that cascade over glistening rocks, wet and slick with flowing moisture. Soggy roots squish underneath trekkers' feet, saturated with copious hydration from the seemingly constant rainfall. Carpet-thick moss spreads up tree trunks and over downed logs, velveting the natural world in a shade of green that can only be found in a box of crayons. Mushrooms sprout up from the depths of the damp earth, happy little toadstools that found their forever home in a land of rain and forest. Light beams occasionally penetrate the dense canopy, filtering warmth between the fluttering leaves and reaching down for the plant life in an effort to offer life-sustaining sunshine. Yes, this trail was perfect for the Wylder Goods backpacking trip.

The group had mixed experience. A few of the women were lifelong backpackers with ample experience and knowledge in the backcountry whereas others were novices, without any idea how to pack a backpack or even poop in the woods. Jainee and Lindsey explained the basics and helped the women feel as comfortable as possible before embarking on the journey. Once their packs were loaded and shoelaces tied, the crew of women hit the trail.

Early October is a gentle season in that Mother Nature is in a state of transition. The blazing hot days make way for the brisk evenings, and cool rains and brief snowstorms occasionally trump days full of sun. This transition appeared to be the theme of the trip.

Jainee suffered. Unsure as to what she ate, it was almost as if a severe case of Montezuma's Revenge had ravaged her intestines, rendering her ill and weak—and very explosive. From day one, she needed to drop her pack and abruptly dart off-trail to take care of business whenever her stomach cramped and contorted in that desperate and painful way. Obviously it was less than ideal, and she was certainly miserable, but she valiantly toughed it out in the name of their new company. After all, these women had supported her dream; who cared if she was a little sick?

They continued on to Hanks Lake, laughing and joking with each other as the novice backpackers fell into step with the experienced. Everyone grew more comfortable with hiking and the trail and had just settled into a comfortable pace when they received another curveball in the form of a black bear.

As the group approached the lake, they lifted their eyes to admire the glistening surface and celebrate their arrival. But there on the other side was a lumbering black bear, gigantic and burly as he crashed his way through the underbrush in search of snacks. He barely acknowledged their existence, but it didn't matter. For the women who were tentatively dipping their toes into the outdoor world, this rumbling mammal was far

Watching the sunset at Pamelia Lake WYLDER GOODS

too much to mentally process. Rather, he was downright terrifying. The ladies took off pell-mell, running toward camp to hide in the safety of their small tents. Eventually everyone calmed down and smiled about their massive, plodding friend, but his appearance certainly exacerbated the nerves of a few.

The final straw came the following morning. The women bedded down, Jainee with her stomach flu and many others dreaming of gigantic black bears wandering through camp. They awoke with the sun only to realize that summer's warmth had transitioned overnight; the entire landscape was covered in snow.

As the morning waxed on, the snow melted into moisture and the gray sky loosed cold, fat drops onto the already chilled and damp women. Jainee and Lindsey knew that it was time to chat. They called a group discussion.

How is everyone feeling? Are you cold? Are you happy? How comfortable are you? Are we still having fun?

In the end, the women called an audible. They hiked back to the trailhead a day early and drove to nearby hot springs, sufficiently happy in the bubbling hot water while they watched salmon spawning in the nearby stream.

The Kickstarter trip to Hanks Lake was wrought with beautiful surprises, but that is how Mother Nature occasionally plays her cards. For Jainee and Lindsey the trip encompassed everything they love about the wilderness, and about business. Every

Cozying up to a campfire WYLDER GOODS

BACKPACKING TIPS FOR BEGINNERS

If you are preparing to hit the trail for the first time, take a look at the following tips. Have fun!

- **Choose a simple destination.** No need to tackle difficult terrain to complicate things!
- **Plan ahead.** Make sure you have the proper gear, an organized menu, and a system in place so that you can find everything when needed.
- **Learn about LNT.** Leave No Trace etiquette guides backcountry behavior, so be sure you educate yourself on the appropriate dos and don'ts of the wilderness.
- **Don't overpack.** You'll just create an unnecessarily heavy pack that you'll later regret.
- **Carefully find a friend.** It's a great idea to take someone with you with experience so they can help you along the way. Plus, the outdoors loves company!

moment of suffering or struggle is met with a gorgeous sunset or campfire laughter. And that mixed bag of emotions is absolutely what makes the experience such a wild ride.

THE HIKE

Begin at the parking lot at the end of Pamelia Creek Road. The trail ascends very gently through densely wooded old-growth terrain. Meander along Pamelia Creek for the majority of the way to Pamelia Lake, allowing your legs plenty of time to warm up. After a few miles, you will reach a trail junction just before the lake. If you plan to continue directly on to Hanks Lake, take a left and stay on Pamelia Lake Trail. But if you want to spend some time at Pamelia Lake and enjoy the scenery, continue straight on the user trail that runs next to the shoreline. It ends quickly, but Pamelia Lake Trail is much farther from the shore so the views are less optimal.

Regardless, once you decide to continue on to Hanks Lake, maintain the Pamelia Lake Trail that runs along the north side of the lake until the junction with Hunts Creek Trail. Take a right and follow this trail as it wraps along the eastern shore of the lake before continuing upstream. The trail dramatically steepens about 0.5 mile after you leave the shores of the lake, and you will continue to steeply climb until you reach your next trail junction at just over 5,000 feet. You will see a wooden sign here with an arrow pointing left toward Hunts Cove Trail. Take the left and climb another ½ mile or so until you reach Hanks Lake.

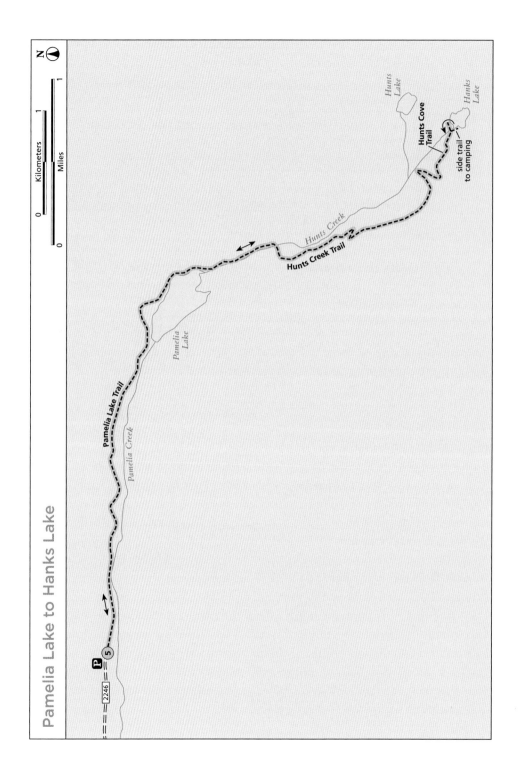

Pamelia Lake to Hanks Lake

N

Kilometers
0   1

Miles
0   1

2246

P

5

Pamelia Lake Trail

Pamelia Creek

Pamelia Lake

Hunts Creek Trail

Hunts Creek

Hunts Cove Trail

Hunts Lake

side trail to camping

Hanks Lake

MILES AND DIRECTIONS

0.0 Begin at the parking lot at the end of Pamelia Creek Road (Forest Road 2246).

2.1 Trail junction; stay to the left to maintain Pamelia Lake Trail or go straight to enjoy the user trail along the lake.

2.3 Trail junction; take a right to catch the Hunts Creek Trail that flanks the east side of the lake.

3.5 The trail dramatically steepens as it climbs the ridge.

5.0 Trail junction; take a left to go to Hanks Lake.

5.3 A small side trail jogs to the right; take this to head to Hanks Lake and find camping.

CAROLINE GLEICH

Grandeur Peak
Salt Lake City, Utah

Caroline Gleich is a professional ski mountaineer, endurance athlete, and environmental activist who hails from Minnesota. However, she was 15 years old when a Utah avalanche killed her half-brother, Martin. As a result, her family picked up their roots and relocated to Salt Lake City in an effort to help Martin's widow and unborn child. In her new surroundings, Caroline pursued her dreams by skiing as much as possible. One year later, when she was 16, she spotted the *Chuting Gallery* on a coffee table at a friend's house, changing her life. Written by Andrew McLean, the *Chuting Gallery* is a guide to the 90 gnarliest ski descents in the Wasatch. Martin perished in one of these descents, so the book stirred something in Caroline that she held onto for the next decade. Finally, in 2012, Caroline officially embarked upon her journey to become the first female to complete the

Caroline Gleich RYAN VOIGHT

Chuting Gallery, a feat she accomplished in 2017. Currently, she is sponsored by Patagonia, Leki, KEEN, Julbo, Clif Bar, Pret Helmets, and Movement Skis.

Though one of the most easily reachable peaks in the Wasatch, Grandeur Peak isn't without its challenges. With over 2,000 feet of vertical gain, this hike is a quad-buster for even the most avid of hikers. People are prevalent on this trail, but can you blame them? The bang-for-your-buck factor is high on Grandeur, with a relatively quick hike time (compared to other Wasatch peaks) and outstanding 360-degree summit views.

Nearest Town: Salt Lake City

Getting There: From Salt Lake City, catch I-80 E to exit #128 for I-215 S/Belt Route. Drive for 1.4 miles until exit #4 for 3900 S. Take a left on 3900 S before taking your first left onto Wasatch Boulevard. Then take your first right onto Mill Creek Road. Drive 3.2 miles until you see the trailhead on the left.

Trailhead: Church Fork Trailhead **GPS:** N40 41.850', W111 44.580'

Fees and Permits: The route begins in Mill Creek Canyon, which is a fee area. A tollbooth is located 1.5 miles up the canyon and users pay the $3 fee upon exiting.

Trail Users: Hikers, trail runners

Elevation Gain: 2,387 feet

Length: 5.4 miles RT (out-and-back)

Approximate Hiking Time: Half Day

Difficulty: Strenuous

Insider Info: This is an exposed, sunny hike—especially up high—but the views more than make up for the hot terrain. Beware of rattlesnakes!

Managing Agency: Uinta-Wasatch-Cache National Forest

EXPERIENCING IT

Most people envision the steep climbs uphill to be the worst part of any hike, but for Caroline Gleich it was the opposite. By the downhill of her third lap on Grandeur Peak, the pain was becoming so excruciating that Caroline wondered if she could make it any farther. Her joints ached with every knee-pounding downhill stride and her quads burned as they attempted to stabilize her legs. *Thud, thud. Thud, thud.* Every

Caroline Gleich in her element MIKE McMonagle

step caused another shock to run through her body and she briefly questioned her decision to be here. Did she have another lap in the tank?

It was a chilly Saturday in February with highs for the day hovering in the single digits. Thick gray clouds filled the sky, with fleeting patches of warm light bursting through the seams before quickly disappearing among the darker shadows of storm clouds. Snow covered the ground like an unwelcome guest. It hadn't been a great snow year in Salt Lake City, so the stuff that hung around was drab and dingy from a long season void of refreshers and refills. The infamous cough-inducing inversion hung in the air like an impermeable shroud, an unpleasant reminder of why they were hiking. This was the eighth annual Running Up For Air (RUFA), and they were trekking because of this very inversion.

Scheduled in February thanks to the notoriously poor air quality that month, RUFA is an endurance trekking/running event that fundraises money to support the fight for better air in the Wasatch. As an environmental activist and endurance athlete, Caroline signed up to run. The goal of RUFA is simple: Opt in for either the 6-hour, 12-hour, or 24-hour challenge, and then run/hike as many laps of Grandeur Peak as possible in your allotted time. This was Caroline's first RUFA, and she registered for the 12-hour event. This meant she would begin each lap at the group campsite at 5,780 feet, make her way to the summit of Grandeur Peak at 8,299 feet as quickly as possible, and then descend back to the group campsite. Wash, rinse, repeat for 12 hours.

The first and second laps were full of smiles. The cold air felt good as her heart rate increased, externally cooling her body while she pushed her

Trekking up Grandeur in the snow ROB LEA

physical boundaries. Caroline found her rhythm while she hiked up, meditating to the constant pattern of her footsteps and trekking pole clicks. Her breathing steadied as she carefully watched the terrain change beneath her feet. The frozen dirt at the bottom gave way to slushy snow as she climbed higher toward the peak, nabbing each summit in ankle-deep snow.

She knew she was growing tired as she summited her third lap, but she certainly wasn't expecting the pain to kick in as strongly as it did on the descent. Her joints screeched at her as the impact of every step shot up through her core. But Caroline is a professional who is accustomed to long days on the trail, packed full of questionable choices and emotionally trying moments. Prepared for such discomfort, Caroline resorted to the tested tactic she uses on every multi-hour expedition that calls for numerous hours of repetitive motion: pep talks.

Ignoring the excruciating pain, Caroline internally reminded herself of her good fortune. "*You signed up for this,*" she told herself. "*You chose to be here; this is your choice. This is your choice.*" She pounded downhill from Grandeur's summit, repeating those words to herself as many times as needed, occasionally matching the cadence to her footsteps to help pound out a rhythm. Sometimes she verbalized them aloud if she needed the added boost. "*It's a privilege and luxury to be doing this, to have access to the excess calories and time,*" she reminded herself.

Taking in the views on the descent ROB LEA

The self-help worked long enough to pry her away from the food and warmth at base camp, an almost masochistic concept. Designed to help athletes by providing what they need in terms of calories and comfort, base camp also taunts them at every turnaround. Caroline knew she could stop whenever she wanted, rip off her shoes, and collapse into a cozy chair, but that would be missing the point. Instead, she reached the bottom of her third lap, grabbed some snacks, and headed back out once again. She knew the pain would increase tenfold once she summited and turned downhill, but in the meantime, she could enjoy the climb. After all, she was here at this event to push her limits and find out what she capable of on that particular day.

Turns out, on February 10, 2018, Caroline was capable of a whopping four laps up and down Grandeur Peak for a total of 25 miles and 10,800 feet of vertical gain over the span of 12 hours. But her success didn't come without consequences, a fact she unfortunately discovered later that evening. She awoke in the middle of the night, her legs viciously cramping and knotting thanks to the day's excess usage. Tears streamed down her face as she suffered through the worst of it. Thankfully, she maintains a great perspective through all of the discomfort, constantly reminding herself of the bigger picture. Why do this?

For Caroline, it's about community acknowledgement of a bigger problem that is larger than any one person. A single individual can't clean up the air problem in Salt Lake City, and it will certainly take more work and effort than a single RUFA event to make a difference. But if you add up all the volunteers, race coordinators, and participants, you are looking at a large number of people banding together for the environment and fighting to protect her in the best way they know how. It's inspiring, it's powerful, and it's energizing.

And that is how change begins.

12,000 YEARS OF HISTORY: MILL CREEK CANYON

These days, Mill Creek Canyon (home to the Church Fork Trailhead) is packed full of outdoor enthusiasts hiking, climbing, mountain biking, and trail running throughout the Wasatch Range. But what many of these outdoorists may not know is that they are merely the most recent in a long line of civilizations to utilize this canyon for a variety of purposes.

The earliest people believed to exist in this area, Paleo-Indians, arrived as early as 12,000 years ago. While we don't have concrete evidence that these people explored Mill Creek Canyon, we know that it is highly likely due to their nomadic nature. They were hunting nomads who followed their food during the late Ice Age. The Paleo-Indians were followed by the Archaic Peoples, another nomadic hunting people who lived in the area from 8,000–4,000 BC. They also gathered their food, leading us to believe they existed here during a hotter, drier period of time. The Fremont Ancestral Puebloans are the third group we believe lived in this Mill Creek area, from 400 BC–700 AD. Like previous cultures they were hunters, but the Fremont Ancestral people also used an impressive agricultural system to feed themselves. Finally, from 700 AD to the 1700s came the people we know as direct ancestors to modern Utah tribes. Modern tribes formed around the 1700s and exist into the present day. Two of these tribes, the Utes and the Shoshone, frequented Mill Creek for its hunting opportunities, even referring to it as "rock trap" thanks to one of their hunting skills that caused elk and deer to fall off the cliffs.

The early 1800s saw the next group of people arrive in Mill Creek: trappers. These fur trappers and traders came from Santa Fe. One of them was the famed Etienne Provost, the French-Canadian fur trapper who is the namesake for the city of Provo, as well as the river and canyon.

Not long after the trappers came the Latter-Day Saint pioneers. Arriving in 1847, these faith-based settlers found their new homes near the various river drainages exiting the Wasatch. One of the more popular places to settle was near the mouth of Mill Creek Canyon thanks to its access to water, timber, and granite. For this reason, almost 85 percent of Utah's population now lives within 15 miles of the Wasatch with the majority of them living to the west.

THE HIKE

The trail begins at the north end of the Church Fork picnic area, where the winding road ends at a small parking area. This is the official trailhead and if you begin your mileage sooner, it will be longer than printed. From here, follow the stream until you come to an intersection with the Pipeline Trail; veer slightly left and then take a quick right to stay on Grandeur Peak Trail.

Grandeur Peak

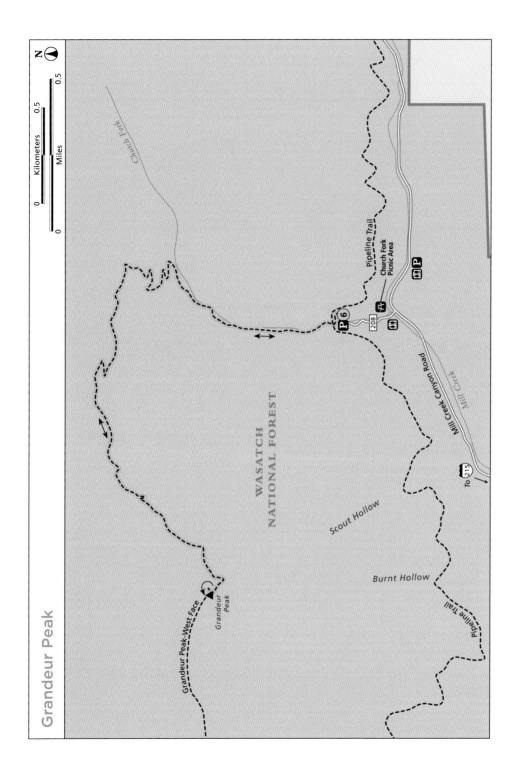

The path climbs gradually through the trees; enjoy the shade as it dwindles by the time you arrive at the steep switchbacks. Continue switchbacking up, ignoring the small trail that darts east; that goes to Church Fork Peak and isn't the goal. Instead, stay on the Grandeur Peak Trail until you reach a small saddle with views of the city to your north and Grandeur Peak to the west. From here, ascend the ridge toward, but don't be tricked by, the false summit that looms in front of you. Continue past the juniper trees and wrap south of the actual summit before climbing the final section to the apex of the peak.

MILES AND DIRECTIONS

0.0 Start at the north side of the Church Fork picnic area.

0.1 Intersection with the Pipeline Trail; veer left and then take a quick right.

0.8 Switchbacks begin climbing.

2.2 Arrive at the saddle.

2.7 Reach the summit. Turn around and retrace your steps to the trailhead.

Spring is in the air on Grandeur. RYAN VOIGHT

SARAH HERRON

Half Dome via the Mist Trail
Yosemite Valley, California

Colorado native Sarah Herron first shot to fame through her participation in season 17 of the wildly popular TV show, *The Bachelor*. She was the first contestant with a physical disability as she was born with Amniotic Band Syndrome, which left her without the lower half of her left arm. She quickly became an audience favorite and went on to appear in the spinoff, *Bachelor in Paradise*. But, unlike many other

Sarah Herron DYLAN H. BROWN

contestants from the show, Sarah opted to use her fame for well-meaning endeavors. This is how she created her nonprofit, SheLift.

Founded in 2016, SheLift is dedicated to empowering girls with physical differences to improve self-confidence through the healing and transformative powers of the outdoors. Through once-in-a-lifetime outdoor retreats, girls are afforded the opportunity to experience new skills while enjoying comfortable and uplifting surroundings. Through her work with SheLift, she wants girls to know that she will be there as their friend to accompany them throughout their journey.

Don't let the name fool you: Half Dome isn't half of anything as this is a physically demanding and strenuous full-day hike. But it can be argued that this hike should be on any hiker's life list as the rewards are innumerable, with spectacular views of Yosemite Falls, Nevada Fall, and of course, Half Dome itself. The nightcap to this challenging hike is the slightly terrifying final section known as the Cables, a set of steep bolted cables that scale the final 60-degree section of rock before dumping you on the summit. While this section can be unnerving, it's a rewarding conclusion to a memorable day.

Nearest Town: Yosemite Village, Yosemite National Park, California

Getting There: Once they are in Yosemite Valley, the epicenter of Yosemite National Park, most people begin this hike from Happy Isles, shuttle stop #16 on the Valley Shuttle. Parking can be found at Half Dome Village (¾ mile from Happy Isles) or at the Trailhead Parking (½ mile from Happy Isles). From there, walk along the road or catch the shuttle until you see the trailhead.

Trailhead: Happy Isles **GPS:** N37 44.079', W119 33.950

Fees and Permits: To gain entrance to Yosemite National Park, there is a $35/vehicle fee (unless you already possess a National Parks Pass). Additionally, there are Half Dome permits for day hikers. These are required 7 days per week when the cables are up, which is usually from Memorial Day weekend to Columbus Day weekend. A maximum of 300 hikers/day are allowed and these permits are granted via two different lottery systems. The preseason lottery spans from Mar 1–Mar 31 and grants 225 of the 300 daily permits. This lottery is administered via recreation.gov and costs $20: $10 for a nonrefundable processing fee and $10 once you are granted a permit. The daily lottery grants 50 permits per day during hiking season with an application period of two days prior to the hike. The fees are the same for the daily lottery as for the preseason lottery. Finally, if you are backpacking (including spending the night in

Little Yosemite Valley), you should apply for your Half Dome permit when you make a wilderness permit reservation ($5 nonrefundable processing fee + $5 fee once you receive the permit). If Half Dome permits are available and it is a reasonable part of your itinerary, you will likely be granted the permit.

Trail Users: Hikers

Elevation Gain: 5,164 feet

Length: 14.8 miles RT (out-and-back)

Approximate Hiking Time: One Day

Difficulty: Strenuous

Insider Info: The Cables portion of Half Dome is arguably the most infamous thanks to the sheer drop and slick nature of the rock. Don't panic, but it is important to take the advisory warnings seriously. The granite is very slick from years of wear and some people opt to rope up during this section (especially if they are hiking with children). But this section is very rewarding because once you complete the Cables, you are on the top of Half Dome!

Managing Agency: Yosemite National Park

EXPERIENCING IT

Sarah Herron will be the first to tell you she doesn't have all the answers. In fact, she is quick to remind people that she is still learning and working on her own self-confidence, especially in relation to outdoor adventure. It was a mere three years ago that Sarah finally decided to jump into the proverbial deep end by tackling

Preparing for a big day DYLAN H. BROWN

Soaking in the view at Vernal Fall
DYLAN H. BROWN

solo day hikes in the hills near Los Angeles where she lived. At first she was absolutely intimidated and scoured every blog she could find, looking for basic details like how many granola bars she should pack and what type of electrolytes she should mix into her water. But over time she gained more confidence and began hiking regularly, enjoying the freedom and mental clarity the fresh air provided her.

During one of her many detailed research sessions online, Sarah came across Half Dome in Yosemite National Park. She quickly became enamored with the strenuous hike, watching YouTube footage and incessantly reading recaps of others who completed the iconic route. She didn't know how or when, but she set a goal for herself: She would hike Half Dome.

She roped in as many friends as possible to apply for permits, knowing that it was a competitive process and she stood a better chance with more applications. Fortunately, they were granted permits, so Sarah found herself standing at the trailhead, printed map instructions from her favorite blog in hand, staring up at the hike looming before her.

She and her friend began hiking while Sarah mentally prepared herself for the day's challenge. She had never hiked such a long route before, let alone one as arduous and physically demanding as Half Dome. Her quads screamed as she climbed the stone staircases, admiring waterfall after waterfall. Eventually, she reached Sub Dome and she found her nerves escalating as they neared the crux of the hike: the Cables.

Sarah stood at the bottom of the towering granite slab, looking at the final 400 feet of her journey. Multiple people dotted the wall like little ants, arms and legs splayed between the cables as they slowly crept up toward the summit. As she

Sarah looking up at The Cables
DYLAN H. BROWN

watched the other hikers fully exert themselves to climb the Cables, Sarah felt the familiar self-doubt creep back into her mind. *What was she thinking trying to hike Half Dome? How could she even consider such a hike with only one hand?*

Nevertheless, Sarah's friend encouraged her to ignore her fear. The two of them began climbing the Cables, bit by bit and inch by inch. They slowly crept up the wall of granite, methodically approaching each rung on the ladder with a focused concentration usually reserved for a competitive game of chess.

But then, about half way up the rock face, Sarah panicked. She experienced a full-blown breakdown unlike anything she had previously experienced on a hike. Paralyzed with fear, she clung to the side of the Cables, completely immobilized and unable to make forward or backward progress. She was simply stuck. Her mind whirled with all of the potential consequences of the hike, and her mounting terror continued to force down any semblance of rational thought.

Just when she thought her hysteria would consume her, a friendly voice floated up from below: *Do you want me to help you get to the top?* Sarah, filled with fear and still refusing to look at the drop below her, acquiesced to the unknown fatherly figure without ever looking at him. She nodded her head and whimpered: *Yes, please.*

Bolstered by her guardian angel, Sarah continued upward while listening to the soothing conversation offered by her new-found friend. He provided guidance on where to place her hands and feet while telling her stories about his daughter who was away at college. Sarah carefully listened to the gentle man's tales. Before she realized what happened, both she and the kind stranger were standing atop Half Dome. She promptly burst into tears.

WHAT HAPPENED TO HALF DOME?

Despite its misleading name, Half Dome was never whole. Contrary to what many think, Half Dome sported a matching half on the smooth flat side. However, it was much larger than the granite tower we see today. Millions of years ago, a large vertical crack exposed itself when glaciers flowed by and mashed underneath the dome. In the process, the glaciers carried away roughly 20 percent of the granite while other chunks broke off in later years. In reality, the dome you see today is merely 80 percent of what it once was!

For Sarah, her Half Dome accomplishment encapsulates everything she hopes to bring to the girls who participate in SheLift retreats. If it hadn't been for the helpful and supportive words of the lovely man on the Cables, Sarah doubts she would have summited Half Dome. To date, this hike is one of her proudest achievements, and her only wish is that she can bring that same feeling of confidence and pride to other girls.

THE HIKE

Beginning at the Happy Isles bus stop, you will first encounter a paved trail that gradually gains in elevation as it climbs from the trailhead. Cross the Happy Isles bridge and take a right onto Mist Trail, where you will soon encounter a large mileage marker sign. This is the official start of the hike, as well as the beginning of the John Muir Trail. Continue hiking uphill until you reach the Vernal Fall Footbridge. There is a water fountain here, as well as flush toilets. This will be the last opportunity for running water, so fill up if needed. After the footbridge, the trail climbs steeply towards Vernal Fall. The stone staircase is frequently slick with moisture and mist, a constant reminder as to the origins of the trail's name. Once you reach the fall, snap a photo and continue up through a shady forest and multiple stone staircases. One mile after Vernal Fall, you will reach the Nevada Fall area. You will also reach a trail junction; take a left if you want to continue directly to Half Dome. If you plan on returning via Mist Trail, it may be worth a short detour to the right to check out the viewpoint from the very top of Nevada Fall. But this is your choice as there is still plenty of hiking to go.

From the junction the trail levels out for about a mile, granting you a bit of reprieve. At this point you are now on the John Muir Trail, so follow signage for this trail as you hike through various trail intersections. Soon, the trail points upward and you will once again begin steeply climbing. At roughly 5.5 miles, you will reach a trail intersection with a metal sign; this is where Half Dome and John Muir Trail split. To continue to Half Dome, stay to the left. Once you reach this sign, you know there

Half Dome via the Mist Trail

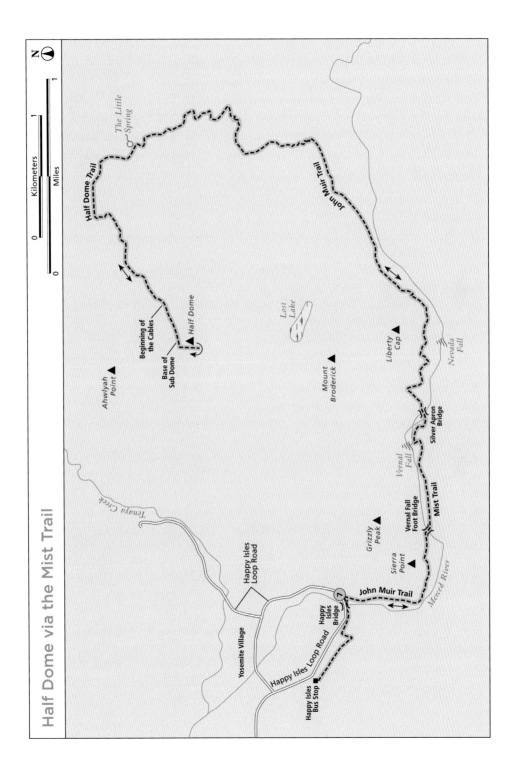

N

Kilometers

Miles

Half Dome Trail

The Little
Spring

John Muir Trail

Beginning of
the Cables

Half Dome

Ahwiyah
Point

Base of
Sub Dome

Lost
Lake

Mount
Broderick

Liberty
Cap

Nevada
Fall

Silver Apron
Bridge

Vernal
Fall

Tenaya Creek

Grizzly
Peak

Vernal Fall
Foot Bridge

Mist Trail

Happy Isles
Loop Road

Sierra
Point

Merced River

John Muir Trail

Yosemite Village

Happy
Isles
Bridge

Happy Isles Loop Road

Happy Isles Bus Stop

are only 2 miles to go. Hike uphill for roughly another mile before reaching the base of Sub Dome, the entrance to the final stretch. There are frequently rangers here to check your permit, so have it accessible. Hike the slow-going steep staircase etched into the rock, eventually reaching the top of Sub Dome with your first view of Half Dome. From here, you will embark on your final task of the climb: the Cables. Using the near-vertical bolted cable ladder, climb the slick wooden steps to the top of Half Dome. This stretch is a two-way street with uphill climbers on the right and downhill hikers on the left, so use caution. Once you have reached the top of the Cables, you are standing on Half Dome. Return to the trailhead the same way you came.

MILES AND DIRECTIONS

0.0 Beginning at the Happy Isles bus stop, follow the path to the Happy Isles Bridge.

0.6 Take a right and locate the large sign that indicates the beginning of the John Muir Trail.

1.4 You've reached Vernal Fall Footbridge and the last water fountain and restroom on the trail.

1.5 Trail junction; stay to the left.

1.6 Trail junction; keep left to stay on Mist Trail or take a right to opt for the longer and more gradual John Muir Trail.

2.0 You've reached Vernal Fall.

2.2 Pass over the Silver Apron Bridge.

3.0 Trail junction with the John Muir Trail; stay to the left as the trail levels out.

3.5 Trail junction; stay to the right.

4.0 A series of trail junctions; continue to stay to the left.

4.2 The trail begins steeply climbing again.

5.4 Trail junction; stay to left on Half Dome Trail as the John Muir Trail jogs right. You have 2 miles left.

5.8 An occasional little spring lives here if you are in desperate need of water.

6.8 You've reached the base of Sub Dome. Your permits may be checked here.

7.2 The beginning of the Cables.

7.4 You've reached the summit of Half Dome. Return to Yosemite Village via the same trail.

SHANTI HODGES
Rowena Plateau
The Dalles, Oregon

Shanti Hodges is a writer, author, and founder of Hike It Baby, a nationwide non-profit dedicated to getting families with children from birth to school age outside. At present, Hike It Baby has 298 branches, 685 ambassadors and 180,000 participating families in the United States, as well as 30 more international branches spread across the globe.

Shanti Hodges with her son, Mason BECCA HARRISON

Shanti is the author of *Hike It Baby: 100 Awesome Adventures with Babies and Toddlers*, as well as the brains behind the podcast, *Hiking My Way to Happiness*. She is also the visionary behind Family Forest Fest, an annual kid-focused weekend festival in Oregon.

This flat and mellow stroll over the Rowena Plateau is a great option for families with children, or even if you just want to get out, sniff some wildflowers, and enjoy the fresh air. Located in the Tom McCall Nature Preserve, the Nature Conservancy has done an exceptional job of preserving the flowers and monitoring rare plant populations. Truly, if springtime wildflower walks are something you and your family enjoy, this trail is tough to beat.

Nearest Town: The Dalles, Oregon

Getting There: From I-84 E, take exit #69 for Mosier via US 30. From there, follow the Columbia River Highway into Mosier. Continue driving east for 7 miles; you will see a turn on your right with a sign that says "Rowena Crest."

Trailhead: Rowena Crest Trailhead **GPS:** N45 40.973', W121 18.124'

Fees and Permits: None

Trail Users: Hikers, trail runners

Elevation Gain: 278 feet

Length: 2 miles RT (out-and-back)

Approximate Hiking Time: Half Day

Difficulty: Easy

Insider Info: Hands down, the best time to visit this trail is in the spring when lupine and balsamroot are showing off their colorful blooms. While this is a family-friendly trail, be aware of the poison oak! No dogs allowed.

Managing Agency: Nature Conservancy of Oregon

EXPERIENCING IT

It all began in 2013 with the birth of Shanti's son, Mason. Shanti was an older mother—41 years old—when Mason was born and she struggled finding a new order to her life. With a husband who often traveled for work, she was frequently left on her own with the new baby. While understanding, her friends were *not* baby people.

And, even if they were, they moved on from that stage of life. Convinced she would sink into postpartum depression and desperately trying not to sit around at home by herself, Shanti identified the one thing that would help lift her spirits during this confusing and chaotic period of life. She took to the trails.

In retrospect, she arrived at that first trail both ill equipped and over prepared. She brought close to everything she could find from Mason's room, ironically confident that more was definitely better. She lugged the stroller along too, unsure of where else she could put her three-week-old kiddo. As she muscled the wheeled contraption up the trail, struggling to navigate over rocks and around shrubs, she thought to herself, *"There has to be a better way."*

While that first hike was not pretty, it was effective. Convinced fresh air was the cure for her mental and emotional ailments, Shanti continued hitting the trail with Mason. She learned more about the gear, eventually picking up an actual child carrier to use in place of the bumbling stroller. She returned home from every hike reenergized and happy with her place in the world, a content feeling that became the catalyst for the next excursion. But she eventually wanted company to join her on these hikes, so she began networking. At first she invited a few families to come along. When those hikes went well, she invited

Shanti's son Mason enjoying the flowers on the plateau BECCA HARRISON

a few more. Over time her invitee list grew longer and longer and she realized more and more families were meeting up with her at the trailhead. Some were experienced while others were novices simply looking for a support system. But the common thread was singular: Everyone wanted to be outside in the sunshine with their family.

These group hikes took on a mind of their own. What began as Shanti struggling along a trail with a stroller morphed into four or five different families all laughing and joking as they sauntered up the hillside with kids of varying ages scattering to the four winds. The pro hikers in the group expounded on their knowledge—this is how Shanti learned to nurse hands-free while hiking—and the beginners filled in the gaps with enthusiasm and excitement for what was to come. It was an imperfect, unstructured system, but it worked.

Eventually, Shanti realized that she was onto something grander than just the occasional hike with friends. With her background in web development, she used her middle-of-the-night nursing sessions with Mason to build a website. Once formalized, Hike It Baby burst onto the scene. The numbers of involved families grew from a dozen in 2014 to those in a handful of states in 2015. Now, in 2018, Hike It Baby is set to support close to 200,000 families over the span of the year, and the numbers continue to rise. The organization may have started as a means for Shanti to cope with the isolation and confusion that came with her new role as a mama, but it evolved into so much more. Her personal solution has become a saving grace for new mothers around the country. These families show up at the trailhead nervous and uncertain but walk away confident and excited thanks to the new adventure that is a Hike It Baby hike.

The day at Rowena Plateau was the *perfect* Hike It Baby day.

The sun rose high in the sky, sending comfortable warmth down on the group of parents and children walking along the trail. It was in the mid-70s, so everyone

Soaking in the views JENNIFER CAMPBELL

FIVE TIPS FOR HIKING WITH A CHILD

- Pick a short trail with lots of features for kids like trees, stumps to climb on, a creek, or a waterfall.
- Bring plenty of snacks that your toddler enjoys. Don't bring things you think they *should* eat; bring what they really *will* eat. Hiking with hangry babies is less than fun.
- Invest in a good child carrier. As your baby grows, the carrier you need changes, so don't get hung up on just one carrier. Experiment.
- Always bring a tether for the favorite pacifier or toy! It will be a *long* hike if you lose that special item.
- Focus on the moment. Adjust to moving slow on some days, and don't be surprised if you don't get past the first mud puddle. Any forward progress is a victory.

stripped down to breathable footwear and short-sleeved shirts, but it wasn't so hot that sweat poured off their faces. The gorge was lush and verdant; everything was so green that it was tough to discern where one shrub ended and another began as the twisted and gnarled branches wound together in a mass of confusion. Wildflowers popped off, filling the plateau with yellow buttercups and colorful lupine. The dots of color were so bright that it almost seemed as if someone had dumped a basket of Easter eggs in the grass and left them there for intrepid explorers to find.

And the children were happy. *So happy.* As with most Hike It Baby hikes, there were at least seven or eight kids joining in for the event, but you wouldn't know they were strangers by watching them. From the trailhead, the eight children immediately latched onto each other in that familiar way that only comes with the unadulterated innocence of youth. They held hands in excitement, creating an eager support system that ensured they would have friendly company as they voyaged down the trail together. Occasionally, one or two would break away as they elatedly ran off to explore a new discovery, but they always returned to one another, giddy with their findings and overjoyed to have other children to join in the experience. There is comfort in shared excitement and these kiddos were downright euphoric.

The parents hiked along behind the jubilant pack of kids, smiling as the group meandered along the trail. The Hike It Baby crew eventually reached the first pond—Rowena Pond—where two of the kids immediately darted to the small body of water. "THERE ARE FROGS IN THE WATER!" exclaimed one of the boys. As if shot from a cannon, each child sprinted to the shore, desperately eager to witness the unique and delightful amphibians in their natural habitat.

Shanti and the kiddos enjoy a perfect day on Rowena Plateau. JENNIFER CAMPBELL

And so it went. It is rare to have a large group of children enamored and entertained for a long stretch of time, but that is exactly what happened at Rowena Pond. The grownups talked with each other, reveling in their uninterrupted adult conversation, while the children watched in wonder as dozens of tiny frogs scampered in and out of the water.

For Shanti, this single memory epitomizes why she founded Hike It Baby in the beginning. The happy children, the fresh air, and the camaraderie among the adults are just a few of the reasons she knew her idea would be successful. And if she had to select a single hike to embody the spirit of her nonprofit, Rowena Plateau is her choice.

To begin with, it's accessible. The trailhead is easy to locate and it is very straightforward to find the correct route. For Hike It Baby, this is crucial since no one wants to be reading a map and searching the horizon while trying to keep her 2-year-old out of traffic. Secondly, and most importantly, the Rowena Plateau trail truly offers fun for the entire family. So often, Shanti finds trails that are considered "family friendly" only

Rowena Plateau

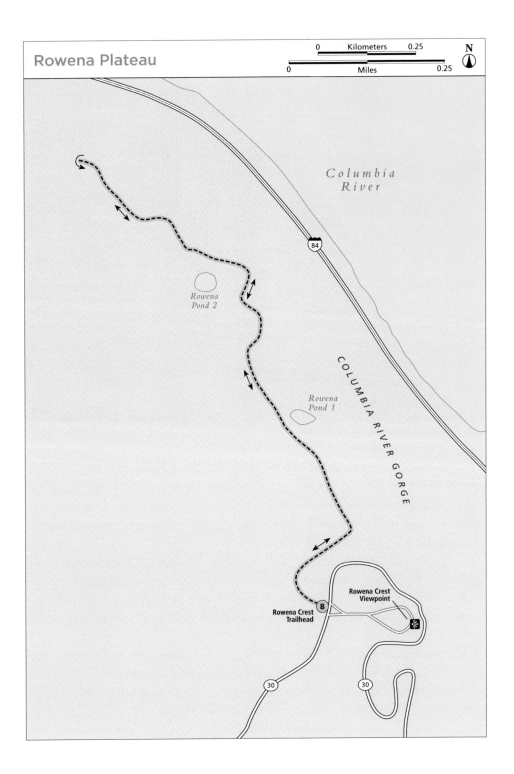

to discover that while they are perfect for enthusiastic kiddos, they are less accessible for elderly grandparents or other family members with physical limitations. "What's the point of finding family-friendly trails when you don't actually mean to include the entire family?" Shanti questions. To this end, Rowena Plateau is perfect. Everyone from infants to octogenarians can find a wilderness respite on this hike and no one gets left behind. Thanks to a wide-open expanse of meadow and limited tree coverage, there isn't anything obstructing the line of sight. Children and adults alike can frolic among the wildflowers and enjoy a day full of fresh air—just the way Shanti and Hike It Baby intended.

THE HIKE

From the Rowena Crest Trailhead, cross the fence stile to enter the plateau. Almost immediately, the trail will gently slope downhill as it does for the entire hike. Yes, this means the return trip is all uphill, but we promise that it isn't too tough! The trail gently and easily curves before gradually winding back in a north–northwest direction; it will continue this trajectory until you turn around. You will pass by two separate "kolk" lakes on your way out, craterlike depressions left over from the floods. After you pass the second, you are close to the end of the trail. On your return trip, don't forget to spend some extra time checking out one of the many side trails that jet off to the east—these will reward you with amazing views of the Columbia River Gorge!

MILES AND DIRECTIONS

0.0 Start in the parking lot for the Rowena Crest Trailhead.

0.1 A trail junction; stay straight to maintain the Rowena Plateau Trail, but jaunting to the right affords you a wonderful view of the gorge.

0.3 Another trail junction. Stay straight.

0.4 You've reached Rowena Pond on your right. Beware of poison oak!

0.5 Another trail junction. Stay straight.

0.6 You've reached the second pond, although it may be difficult to see it through all of the undergrowth.

0.7 Another trail junction; stay straight unless you want to loop back to the car.

1.0 You've reached the end of the trail. Enjoy the views before turning around to retrace your steps back to the car.

KRISTIN HOSTETTER
Franconia Ridge Loop
Franconia, New Hampshire

Kristin Hostetter is the current editor in chief of SNEWS, a digital publication that serves as the outdoor industry's best source for trade news. Prior to this role, she was the long-standing gear editor of *Backpacker Magazine.* Kristin held this position for almost 22 years, helping to pave the way for editorial women by becoming the leading source for outdoor gear testing. She has published four books: *Backpacker Magazine's Complete Guide to Outdoor Gear Maintenance and Repair, Don't Forget the Duct Tape: Tips & Tricks for Repairing & Maintaining Outdoor & Travel Gear, Adventure Journal,* and *Tent and Car Camper's Handbook: Advice for Families and First-Timers.* Additionally, she has appeared on air as a gear expert on NBC's *Today,* CBS's *The Early Show,* and *The Martha Stewart Show,* among others.

Kristin Hostetter ANDREW BYDLON

For many, the Franconia Ridge Loop is the perfect White Mountains hike. It is not easy—quite the opposite!—but the sweat equity is rewarded with jaw-dropping views during the 1.5-mile segment above tree line. It is a very popular hike thanks to its proximity to Boston, so don't expect complete solitude. But the trail never feels overly crowded and there is plenty of space to enjoy the arduous climb. **Note:** *The weather quickly changes in this region, so be double sure you've checked the weather report before hitting the trail. It isn't unusual to begin hiking under bluebird skies only to end up on the ridge with gale-force winds and pelting hail.*

Nearest Town: Franconia, New Hampshire

Getting There: From Franconia, head south on I-93 for just over 8 miles. Take the exit for Lafayette Place Campground. From here, you can catch the walking path and tunnel that goes underneath I-93 and lands you directly at the trailhead on the east side of I-93.

Trailhead: Lafayette Place Parking Area **GPS:** N44 08.515', W71 40.888'

Fees and Permits: None, although reservations and fees are required if you opt to stay in the Greenleaf Hut

Trail Users: Hikers, backpackers, trail runners

Elevation Gain: 3,805 feet

Length: 8.5 miles RT (loop)

Approximate Hiking Time: 1–2 Days

Difficulty: Strenuous

Insider Info: This hike can be done as a large day hike, but cut yourself some slack and turn it into an overnight trip by booking an evening at the AMC Greenleaf Hut. If you complete this loop in a counterclockwise direction, the hut will be after all of the elevation gain, making it an enjoyable respite to kick back, relax, and have a few laughs with your friends.

Managing Agency: White Mountain National Forest

EXPERIENCING IT

Anyone who knows Kristin Hostetter acknowledges her as the tough and smart former gear editor at *Backpacker Magazine* and the current editor in chief at SNEWS. Sharp as a tack, Kristin always asks the right questions. But what many may not realize

A trail runner soaking in the views along Franconia Ridge
JOFFREY PETERS

is that this competitive and driven woman's entire empire stems from this fun fact: She really didn't want to take a college entrance exam.

After moving to Chicago to be with her future husband, the two of them began adventuring up to Wisconsin on the weekends to dabble in the outdoors. First they tried mountain biking, but hated the idea of spending money on hotel rooms every weekend. Camping was the logical succession to avoid regular lodging costs. As a result, the twosome began accumulating the beginnings of a gear closet. To fuel her new hobbies, Kristin frequented a local gear store called Erehwon (nowhere spelled backward). It was like a foreign language at first, but over time she became fascinated with the gear. She loved the specs and materials and design ideas behind the products and as her passion for the outdoors grew, so did her interest in outdoor gear. The seed was planted.

Meanwhile, she was bartending to make ends meet. Knowing that she needed to make some career decisions, she decided graduate school was the best next step. She perused the various program offerings, searching for one that she found intriguing enough for her life's work. Eventually, she stumbled upon a master's in writing program that struck her fancy. She didn't have any grand illusions of being an actual writer, nor did she consider herself to be exceptionally gifted with verbiage. But the courses interested her, and the fine print was the clincher: She didn't need to take the GRE.

She was sold.

Kristin spent the next few years completing her degree while also working part-time at Erehwon after realizing a job there would fund her now-burgeoning outdoor habit. After taking a course at school, Kristin began incessantly pitching stories to *Backpacker*. Filled with ideas, she sent pitch after to pitch to various editors at the magazine, but never received a single response. Ever dauntless, Kristin continued pitching, knowing that one day, something *had* to stick.

And then, she saw it. While aimlessly flipping through the glossy pages of the magazine as had become the norm, she stumbled on an advertisement for a nature writing workshop in Lake Superior. Hosted by the magazine, the workshop was 12 days' worth of kayaking and classroom writing experience with the editors of *Backpacker*. With scholarships available, Kristin used her unbridled energy and never-ending perseverance to secure one.

The workshop was straight out of her dreams. She traveled east to Lake Superior the following spring and spent her days chatting with various editors from the seat of a kayak and her evenings pouring over the material learned in class. She connected mysterious faces with emails that she had repeatedly seen while pitching and established those oh so important relationships. She thrived during the workshop, and returned to Chicago with one thought in her mind: *This is what I want to do. I have to work for this magazine.*

Waterfall along the Falling Waters Trail JULIANNA BRADLEY

She continued pitching once she got home, only now, she knew who she was emailing. Tom, one of her newfound editor friends, recognized her name and scooped her under his experienced wing. He would respond to her emails, explaining to her why a particular concept was not quite right or how she could improve the idea. He continually coached her, providing guidance, encouragement, and tough critiques when needed. Eventually, Tom's tutelage paid off and Kristin earned herself a small, front-of-book assignment. Then she earned another. And another. It was clear Kristin was rabid about this career path, so when an assistant gear editor position opened up shortly thereafter, the magazine made a phone call. Did she want the job? She didn't need to think twice; she hopped on the next flight to Pennsylvania.

Over time, she worked her way up and became the gear editor for *Backpacker*, a position she held for almost 22 years. In an industry where employment revolving doors aren't unheard of, her reign was so commanding that she developed legions of fans, some even creating Facebook groups like the aptly titled *I Want to Hike With Kristin Hostetter*. If ever there were such a thing as outdoor industry royalty, Kristin would have a shot at the title.

As the long-standing queen of the gear realm, Kristin's seniority also afforded her some amazing opportunities and life-list-style trips along the way. As the gear editor, Kristin enjoyed dozens of brand-sponsored outdoor adventures, all in the name of testing gear. She luxuriated in Turkish baths outside of Istanbul and admired the sparkling night sky above Jordan's Petra. She marveled at Tasmania's Wineglass Bay and trekked up and down Switzerland's Via Alpina. But when asked if there is one particular hike that sticks out more than others, none of the exotic media trips made the list. Instead, Kristin opted for something closer to home—literally and figuratively.

Summit of Mt. Lincoln JULIANNA BRADLEY

Facing south from the Old Bridle Path Trail JULIANNA BRADLEY

She observed that many of her girlfriends were marveling at her adventures, always concluding the conversation with, "You should take me one day!" After the third or fourth friend uttered those words, Kristin decided to do something about it. She set about planning a memorable girls' weekend, complete with dirt, sweat, and post-hike meals in a hut. First, she sought out a trail that would blow them away with its

THE GREENLEAF HUT

Overlooking Eagle Lake, this Appalachian Mountain Club (AMC)–owned hut is a backcountry gem. The rewarding views of Mt. Lafayette remind you from whence you came or inspire you for the following day's challenge. Spend a night or two with the hut crew and enjoy the warm atmosphere that comes from being part of their backcountry family. And if you enjoy the hut experience (and the included breakfast and dinner), consider connecting your trek with another hut in the AMC network. Greenleaf is open from May–October with the earlier dates available for self-service season.

beauty. She didn't want a dense, tree-filled walk in the woods; instead, she searched for commanding views that you couldn't find without hard work and physical accomplishment. Next, she searched for the appropriate level of difficulty. Her crew was fit and tough, so she knew the hike needed to challenge them. But she also didn't want to destroy these women by opting for a trail so mentally exhausting that her friends would never want to join her again. Thus, she found the perfect hike: the Mt. Lafayette and Franconia Ridge Loop.

In choosing to hike up the Falling Waters Trail and across the ridge, Kristin and her crew logged the majority of miles in the first day, schlepping their packs up more than 3,500 feet of elevation gain and across the windblown ridgeline, summiting both Mt. Lafayette and Mt. Lincoln. By the time they reached the Greenleaf Hut, they were exhausted, sore, and absolutely exhilarated. Arriving at the cozy and warm shelter was a welcome cherry on top of an already accomplished adventure, but the evening had just begun. The women feasted, enjoying celebratory glasses of wine while toasting to a successful day in the mountains. They shared laughter, smiles, and a litany of trail stories, reveling in the sense of accomplishment that only comes after enduring—and surviving—something physically demanding.

It was a girls' trip to remember. Kristin shared her world with these ladies and in return, she experienced the thing she loved with some of the people she loved most. And there is nothing better than that.

THE HIKE

Begin hiking at the trailhead on the east side of I-93. Almost immediately, you will see a trail sign; follow the arrows for Falling Waters Trail as this is the route you will use to ascend if you opt to complete this loop in the counterclockwise direction (recommended). Hike for a few minutes, passing a small waterfall, before coming to the junction where Falling Waters and Old Bridle Path Trails split. You will stay to the

Franconia Ridge Loop

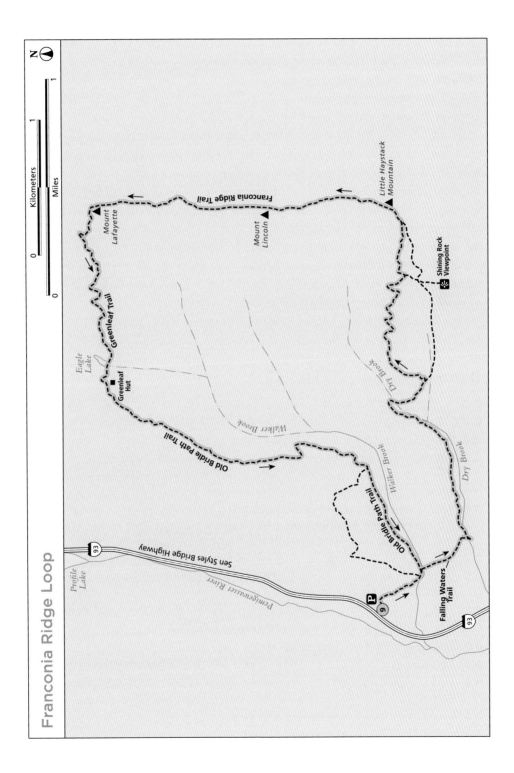

N

Profile Lake

Sen Styles Bridge Highway

Pemigewasset River

93

P
9

Falling Waters Trail

Old Bridle Path Trail

Walker Brook

Dry Brook

Dry Brook

Old Bridle Path Trail

Walker Brook

Greenleaf Hut

Eagle Lake

Greenleaf Trail

Mount Lafayette

Franconia Ridge Trail

Mount Lincoln

Little Haystack Mountain

Shining Rock Viewpoint

Kilometers

Miles

0   1

0   1

right. Cross Walker Brook on a footbridge and begin paralleling Dry Brook, crossing over it multiple times. None of these subsequent crossings have bridges, so be cautious, especially when conditions are extra wet. Eventually the trail moves away from Dry Brook and, after a brief reprieve, begins steeply climbing in earnest. As you near the ridge, you will see a spur trail to the right. This 0.2 mile spur goes to Shining Rock viewpoint, if you are willing to tack on the extra mileage.

Just under ½ mile after the viewpoint spur, you will reach Little Haystack Mountain (4,761 feet). From this junction, connect with the Franconia Ridge Trail by hooking a left. This segment is also part of the Appalachian Trail and a great place to evaluate conditions. If weather looks nasty, it is better to turn around and head back down at this point. If things look good, continue along the ridge, reaching Mt. Lincoln first (5,089 feet), followed by Mt. Lafayette (5,261 feet). Now that your portion of the ridge is complete, you will begin the descent. At the trail junction, take a left to hook up with Greenleaf Trail as it begins rolling down a series of rock staircases and past Eagle Lake on your right. After just over a mile, you will reach the Greenleaf Hut. If you opted to spend an evening here, enjoy!

To continue from the hut, take a left at the next trail junction and catch Old Bridle Path Trail. You will stay on this trail until it returns to the trailhead.

MILES AND DIRECTIONS

0.0 Begin hiking at the trailhead/parking area on the east side of I-93.

0.2 Trail splits; stay to the right to begin on Falling Waters Trail.

1.4 Pass Cloudland Falls on the right side of the trail.

1.7 Falling Waters Trail begins meandering away from Dry Brook.

2.7 Trail junction with the Shining Rock spur trail; stay straight to continue on to the ridge.

3.0 You've reached the summit of Little Haystack Mountain, with amazing views of Mt. Washington and Canon Mountain. This is also the trail junction. Stay left to catch the Franconia Ridge Trail.

3.7 You are now standing on your second peak of the day, Mt. Lincoln.

4.5 Now you are on the summit of Mt. Lafayette, the tallest peak of the day.

4.6 Trail junction; take a left and begin descending on Greenleaf Trail.

5.6 Pass by Eagle Lake on the right side of the trail.

5.7 You've reached the Greenleaf Hut.

5.7 Trail junction; hike left to join up with Old Bridle Path Trail.

8.2 This is a great spot to soak your tired feet in the cool water. You've earned it.

8.5 You've reached the trailhead and your car.

10

JEN HUDAK
Mount Superior via Cardiff Pass
Sandy, Utah

To many, Jen Hudak is one of the greatest female halfpipe skiers of all time. Born and raised in Connecticut, Jen had perseverance and adventure in her blood from the early days, when her father constructed a makeshift rope-tow system so she could ski in their backyard. Her skills progressed, as did her love for halfpipe. Then, in 2004, she found herself standing on her first (of many) podiums at the US Freeskiing Open. From there, she won every professional competition possible: the US Open, World Ski Invitational, Dew Tour, US Nationals, and the X Games. In fact, she racked up

Jen Hudak JEN HUDAK

two gold medals in the 2010 X Games alone, with a grand total of five overall X Games medals. But Jen had set her sights on something even bigger: the Olympics.

Jen strongly believed that halfpipe skiing would make its way to the Olympic stage, and she worked hard to get it there. In fact, many directly credit its debut at the 2014 Sochi Olympics to Jen and all of her efforts over the years. Her dream was to participate in those Olympics, but unfortunately she tore her knee in December 2013 at the qualifier, ending her chances and concluding her ski career.

Today, Jen is a competitive mountain biker, life coach, and writer. She and fellow American freeskier Kristi Leskinen competed on season 30 of *The Amazing Race*, becoming the first team to finish in the top 3 for all 12 legs and finishing with the highest average for any female team in the history of the TV show.

If you are looking to stand atop a classic Wasatch Range peak, look no further. Mount Superior (along with nearby Monte Cristo Peak) towers over Little Cottonwood Canyon and fills the skyline when viewed from nearby Alta Ski Area or Snowbird Resort. This hike is a great way to push your fitness and challenge yourself while tackling steep slopes and somewhat-exposed scrambling near the top. But it is still close to Salt Lake City, so you can return home in time for dinner. **Bonus:** *Hit up Mount Superior in the winter and you'll find yourself a classic ski line.*

Nearest Town: Sandy, Utah

Getting There: From Sandy, catch UT 209 E/Little Cottonwood Road until it connects with UT 210 E. Take a right and drive 8.1 miles up the canyon to the police station and town office.

Trailhead: Alta Sheriff's Office **GPS:** N40 35.581', W111 38.198'

Fees and Permits: None

Trail Users: Hikers, trail runners

Elevation Gain: 2,768 feet

Length: 5.4 miles RT (out-and-back)

Approximate Hiking Time: Half Day–Full Day

Difficulty: Moderate–Advanced

Insider Info: Monte Cristo and Mt. Superior are smack next to each other, but there is some debate over which peak is which. USGS Maps lists the higher summit (11,132 feet) as Mt. Superior, but locals prefer to call the higher peak Monte Cristo and the lower peak Mt. Superior. These directions take you to the first peak, here referred to as Mt. Superior. Regardless, tacking on the additional 15-minute hike from the summit of Mt. Superior over to Monte Cristo is well worth the extra effort.

Managing agency: Uinta-Wasatch-Cache National Forest

EXPERIENCING IT

It was one of those perfect July days in the Wasatch. A bluebird sky filled the horizon, offset by a couple of practically perfect puffy clouds that more closely resembled cotton balls than actual meteorological features. Wildflowers dotted the hillside as cheery indicators of the long days and warm temperatures, their petal-surrounded faces opening and shutting with the dawning and closing of each day. Summer weather is simply made for hiking, and quite a few outdoorists from Salt Lake agreed. Groups of two and three people wearing colorful clothing could be seen scattered up and down the trail, each person huffing and puffing as they tackled the steep terrain that led up to the looming Mount Superior. Jen Hudak was one of these hikers.

This was not the first time Jen had stood atop Mount Superior. In fact, she can barely remember the first time she experienced the magnificent 360-degree views from the summit since she has been up and down the peak so many times. That's what happens when such an iconic trail is minutes from your doorstep. But this warm summer day was memorable in itself: Jen was *hiking* Mount Superior.

For a world-class halfpipe competitor like Jen, life revolved around two things: snow and skis. She literally and figuratively grew up on skis, turning professional when she was merely a teenager. Instead of weekends at the mall, Jen stood atop podium after podium,

Heading up! JEN HUDAK

Scrambling up toward the summit DYLAN H. BROWN

winning various freeskiing competitions. This in itself is telling of her work ethic since there is nothing natural about the sport of halfpipe. Athletes ski down the pipe, launching various tricks and skills off the walls while soaring through the air, before landing and doing it all over again. This type of body control and amplitude calls for

SEX AND THE FEMALE ATHLETE

In 2013, *Freeskier* magazine published an article entitled, "Ten Hottest Women in Freeskiing," highlighting female athletes based on their physical appearance rather than their skiing abilities. Jen directly tackled the problem via a blog post on her website. In "Sex and the Female Athlete," Jen discussed the difficulties female athletes face in an industry focused on their appearances rather than their capabilities. In her article, Jen discussed a *Freeskier* photo shoot she participated in when she was a 17-year-old up-and-comer on the scene. Instead of highlighting her insane amplitude in the halfpipe, the magazine asked her to pose in a bubble bath. As a young athlete, Jen knew exposure was critical at this stage in her career and enjoyed the shoot, but the adult Jen looks back and questions what image she perpetuated.

This wasn't the first time Jen was at the forefront for women's rights in the skiing world. In fact, she fought this battle throughout her professional career. She frequently spoke out against the media coverage of female sports. At the time, 95 percent of on-air time was dedicated to men's sports, and the Dew Tour only showed a highlight reel for the female events versus live on-air coverage for the men's events. Jen vocally supported the X Games since it was one of the few competitions that awarded equal prize money to men and women. Among other reasons, this was why Jen pushed so strongly for halfpipe skiing to be included in the Olympics. Paving the way for future female athletes to compete on the world stage alongside men was a dream come true for Jen, and she continues to be grateful that she played such an integral part in the fruition of that dream.

intense athleticism and nerves of steel due to the inherent risk in the sport; Jen has both. She is naturally gifted and a hard worker; a deadly combo that is tough to beat. But this also meant that everything in life redirected back to skiing. So yes, Jen stood on the summit of Mount Superior many times prior to this vivid July morning, but she always arrived there via skis.

Trekking the peak was so very different than skiing. Coming off her ninth knee surgery (three on her left knee, six on her right), Jen always viewed hiking as a means to an end—it was a great second-choice alternative to skiing thanks to the athletic benefits. Since hiking is such a low-impact sport, surgeons highly recommend the activity post-op to increase fitness and muscle tone without the fear of further damaging joints or ligaments. But for an athlete who routinely landed halfpipe tricks that sent her soaring upwards of 30 feet off the ground, keeping both feet close to terra firma while slowly trekking up a mountain seemed a bit mundane. Until it didn't.

Hiking Mount Superior in July was the first time Jen accepted her body's limitations with grace. She wasn't hiking the trail as a means to anything; in fact, it was the opposite. She wanted to be outside in nature and could think of no better way to enjoy the morning than by hiking the Wasatch's finest with a few good friends. As she steadily worked her way up the mountain, she acknowledged the second change of the day: her hiking poles. Previously, her ego hadn't allowed her to succumb to such a "goofy" addition to her gear kit. But with time comes maturity, and Jen realized she simply didn't care anymore. While her pride still hated relying on the external carbon-fiber support system, she knew it was for the best. She wouldn't be out on the trail with the warm sun reflecting off her face if it wasn't for those very same walking sticks. Rather than dwell on it, she opted for positivity. Halfpipe skiing is notoriously dangerous and

On the last push to the summit DYLAN H. BROWN

Taking a breather with Alta Ski Resort below JEN HUDAK

laden with physical consequences. After years of competition, Jen's body had been through a lot, so now was the time to respect and honor all it had accomplished for her.

She continued upward, hiking through the wildflowers and eventually attaining Cardiff Pass. From there, she scrambled her way westward, along the ridge and up and over a few knobs until she was standing on top of Mount Superior with the entirety of Little Cottonwood Canyon spread out beneath her. It was an entirely different experience challenging the peak on foot rather than skis, but in a way it represented the passing of a torch and the dawning of a new era in her life. For years, Jen was the face of halfpipe skiing, a moniker she decidedly deserved. But now, with her competitive skiing days behind her, the future is still approaching, bright and shiny like a copper penny and full of glittering opportunity. Instead of X-Games podiums she now focuses on helping other professional athletes transition their career paths. Rather than practice a new half-pipe skill she instead engages in public speaking to help others learn how to harness the power of visualization. These days life is full of changes for Jen, and this hike is merely the beginning of what is yet to come. She better hang onto those trekking poles.

Mount Superior via Cardiff Pass

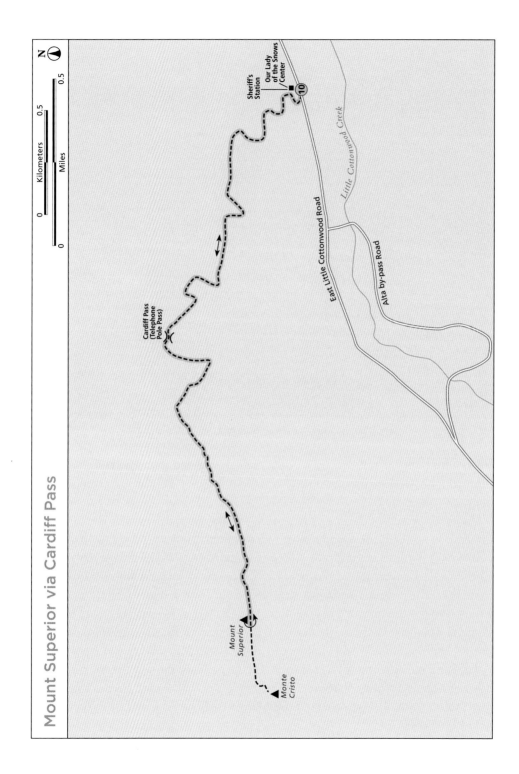

N

Kilometers
0   0.5   0.5

Miles
0   0.5

Mount
Superior

Monte
Cristo

Cardiff Pass
(Telephone
Pole Pass)

Sheriff's
Station

Our Lady
of the Snows
Center

10

East Little Cottonwood Road

Alta by-pass Road

Little Cottonwood Creek

THE HIKE

Begin by walking up the paved road next to Our Lady of the Snows Center, and take your first right. Walk by the Sheriff's Station; the road will curve west as it turns into dirt. Continue to follow the power lines as the road turns back east. Very shortly, the trail splits with an old mining road that forks to the left; take this fork. Work your way up the switchbacks, ignoring all the social trails. Instead, stay on the old mining road. About two-thirds of the way through your hike, you will see an obvious fork; stay to the left. After this split, hike through a meadow and continue upward as the trail grows very steep until you reach Cardiff Pass, aptly known as Telephone Pole Pass thanks to the prominent telephone pole and wires that can be found on the pass. Once here, hang a left (west) and follow the electrical line up the talus-covered ridge. The trail is very steep here in sections, but they are brief. The real scrambling is still to come! Continue to follow the defined path up the ridge as it turns to steep and loose dirt surrounded by talus. This section is not well defined and scrambling will be required, but aim to stay high so you do not lose any of your hard-earned elevation. You will know you've reached the summit when you spot the mailbox with a notebook and pen inside. Don't forget to leave a note!

MILES AND DIRECTIONS

0.0 Begin walking up the paved road next to Our Lady of the Snows Center.

0.1 Take a right as you pass the Sheriff's Station on your left.

0.2 The trail will split; take the mining road to the left and begin climbing.

0.8 You will come to an obvious split in the trail; stay to the left.

1.4 You've reached Cardiff Pass and climbed over 1,300 feet; take a left and hike westward along the ridge.

1.9 The trail grows very steep here and may call for scrambling in sections.

2.6 This is the final push to Mount Superior.

2.7 You've reached the summit; return to the car on the same trail.

RUE MAPP

Sequoia Bayview Trail
Piedmont, California

Rue Mapp is the founder and CEO of Outdoor Afro, a national nonprofit with sixty-two volunteer leaders in twenty-six states whose aim is to connect and organize outdoor enthusiasts around the broader scope of community and leadership in nature. Currently, Outdoor Afro has offices in both Oakland, California, and Washington, DC, but it began with understated roots: as a small blog in 2009. Clearly Rue's message was both needed and well received, because it quickly expanded into a multimedia approach with national sponsorship. This is largely because Rue is clear and concise with a direct message: "Stay in your lane," she likes to say. For Rue, this means expanding diversity and awareness through the lens of the natural world. Rue is an in-demand public speaker and even visited the White House in 2010 as part of the administration's America's Great Outdoors conference. Subsequently, she participated in former First Lady Michelle Obama's "Let's Move" initiative.

In addition to Outdoor Afro, Rue has been listed as one of the most influential African Americans in the country (2012 and 2016) by *The Root*, named one of America's Most Influential Moms by *Family Circle* magazine, and awarded the Outdoor Industry Inspiration Award. She currently sits on the board for the Outdoor Industry Association and

Rue Mapp RUE MAPP

was appointed to the California State Parks Commission in 2014 by Governor Jerry Brown.

The Sequoia Bayview Trail is a great hike for families, kids, and hikers looking for a surprisingly flat trail with ample shade for toasty days. Located in Joaquin Miller Park, the various stands of redwoods are some of the few to flourish in an urban setting, making this a unique hike on the outskirts of the city.

Nearest Town: Piedmont, California

Getting There: From CA 13 S, head southbound until exit #2 for Joaquin Miller Road/Lincoln Avenue. Take a left on Monterey Boulevard followed by another very quick left at the first cross street; this is Joaquin Miller Road. Drive 1.2 miles before taking a left on Skyline Boulevard. Drive roughly ½ mile and you will see the trail on your left.

Trailhead: Sequoia Bayview Trailhead **GPS:** N37 48.477', W122 10.669

Fees and Permits: None

Trail Users: Hikers, trail runners, mountain bikers

Elevation Gain: 280 feet

Length: 2.9 miles RT (loop)

Approximate Hiking Time: Half Day

Difficulty: Easy

Insider Info: Dogs are allowed on this trail, so don't forget your leashed pup! ***Beware:*** There is poison oak on the sides of this trail, so exercise caution.

Managing Agency: City of Oakland

EXPERIENCING IT

To hear Rue Mapp tell it, roots are the source of strength for anything in this world. They ground us to the earth, strong and steadfast with a support system designed to keep us upright during the wayward winds of life. Because of this, the Bayview Sequoia Trail isn't just another hiking trail in a nearby urban park. It's more than that; it's symbolic. Thanks to the redwood trees, this trail has roots. This trail gives you roots.

Redwoods tower over the beginning of the trail. PAULINA DAO

At first glance, the Joaquin Miller Park in the Oakland Hills may not fit the stereotypical image of a pristine wilderness getaway. It is an urban park with little trail signage and the ever-present hum of roaring traffic and overhead airplanes to remind you that you are in a city rather than a protected swath of isolated wilderness. But the park is an oasis in the center of an urban jungle, and it is filled with nature's finest for those willing to visit. The Sequoia Bayview Trail is one such hike.

Dotting the hike are clumps of beautiful coastal redwoods. Joaquin Miller Park isn't the prime location for viewing these stately trees, nor is it the most popular, which adds to the intrigue. But it is a lesson in urban beauty, as the towering trunks stand in stark contrast to the bustling city corridor just beyond the confines of the park. More importantly, these natural wonders teach us lessons about both our history and modern humanity.

Merely saying that redwoods aren't like other trees is akin to saying a house cat is just a touch different than a lion. Commonly referred to as the Giants of the Forest, these fantastically tall trees are the things of fairytales. Stretching so tall into the sky that one has to crank one's neck back just to potentially catch a glimpse of the top, the tallest trees can reach upward of 370 feet in height and 30 feet in width. But these mythical proportions aren't the only reason these trees belong in a fable. They are tough and durable, if not magically so. Bugs cannot touch them and neither can fungi.

As if by sorcery, fire doesn't harm these enchanting beasts either.

Perhaps more heartwarming, however, is the trees' root system. One would imagine that such magnificent trees would require a root system so deep that the anchor roots tapped into the Earth's core, securing these leviathans to the planet with a steel-like strength. That isn't the case. Instead, redwoods believe in community. Their shallow roots sprawl a mere five or six feet beneath the soil but spread up to 100 feet away from the trunk, stretching their rooted arms out in a warm embrace. Instead of latching onto the earth with depth, the redwoods believe in holding each other upright and bolstering each other throughout any of the trials and tribulations that the planet throws at them. Their roots extend far and wide to other redwoods, their family members. They hold on to

The trail practically glows at sunset. PAULINA DAO

each other for support, for nourishment, and for care. Like a band of subterranean soldiers, it is almost as if they hook arms below the soil, uniting together to defend themselves against the world and all of its predators. Redwoods symbolize community.

Redwoods are loyal. Our planet was covered with redwoods thousands of years ago, but these days, coastal redwoods can only be found in one location: on the Pacific Coast of the United States, ranging from Big Sur to southern Oregon. And while they thrive in this location, today's redwoods are merely babies when compared to the old giants that once stood there.

The trail is relatively flat, making it a great option for practically everyone. PAULINA DAO

It was 1849 and San Francisco was inundated with gold miners whose luck had run out. Of course, they needed to work, and realizing that panning for gold was less fruitful than expected, these miners turned to the sure thing: logging. It was a booming industry with money to be made. They joined makeshift logging camps. As more and more towns popped up in the area, logging needs increased. The crews turned their eyes to the redwoods, trees so huge and strong that they must have seemed like a magic construction tool to the tired and worn loggers.

Just like that, old growth redwoods that had been standing for years became new homes in Oakland and San Francisco. Sawmills cropped up everywhere, with men of all backgrounds vying for logging jobs that would bring in the cold, hard cash needed to support their families. This continued for a few years until by 1860, the largest trees were gone and most of the sawmills closed. Even the stumps of the grandest trees had been dug out in an effort to turn them into roof shingles for the homes. The redwoods were nearly destroyed.

These days, Rue frequently thinks of her hometown's history while hiking her beloved Sequoia Bayview Trail. Instead of wandering amidst a sea of old-growth redwoods, Rue instead treks below the canopy of second- and third-generation redwoods. After loggers nearly eliminated the majestic trees, various organizations and governing bodies realized the error of their ways. This is also when second-generation saplings sprouted up, indicating that the redwoods would survive if humanity protected them. Redwoods proved their loyalty and the strength of their family bonds; these are both traits Rue admires in Mother Nature and in humanity. In fact, many of these second-generation saplings are the redwoods that can be found along the Sequoia Bayview Trail today.

For Rue, these determined redwoods embody the resilience and perseverance that she utilizes in her daily work. As a leader of an organization that focuses on African American people, Rue equates the plight of the redwoods to the same challenges that people of color face. She constantly strives to find the appropriate means of showing up and being present in times of conflict, a task that is never easy and almost always

HEALING HIKES

In 2014, the United States saw an increase in high-profile shootings that reignited the debate over racial relations. Some people took to the streets to protest while others lit up social media with arguments and demands for policy reform. Rue did not protest but wondered what her involvement should be. As the leader of Outdoor Afro, she knew she needed an appropriate response, but struggled to find one that suited her and her beliefs. Then one day as she was walking to her car with helicopters flying overhead, it hit her: Stick to what she does best. Stick to nature. And thus, "healing hikes" were born.

The first healing hike included thirty people who headed to the hills outside of Oakland to talk, reflect, and find some peace amidst the noise and chaos of the country's events. They opted to host the hike amidst the redwoods, thankful for the calmness that only the gargantuan trees can bring. Everyone talked about how the violence impacted them and how they wanted to handle the situation moving forward.

From this inaugural event, healing hikes spread. To date, Outdoor Afro has hosted more than fifty healing hikes around the country, each affording individuals the opportunity to reflect and find rejuvenation in contrast with the world's madness. Rue likes to say that nature is accepting, allowing everyone to bring all the parts of themselves to it. For Outdoor Afro, this centers on black joy. "We all need to find joy," says Rue. "We need to hold on to that for each other."

Meandering underneath the canopy RUE MAPP

requires copious amounts of understanding and empathy. Rue appreciates that people look to her for support and guidance and hopes to be the pillar of strength that many need to bolster themselves against.

To do that, the answer is always the same: Return to nature and be like a tree. Be rooted, be connected, and be grounded. Rue likes to believe that if humanity can persevere and find the same loyalty as the redwoods, there will always be hope for the future.

THE HIKE

This lollipop loop trail follows the contour of the land, making it relatively flat and easy to follow. Because of this, the Sequoia Bayview Trail is a wonderful option for beginners who want to gain trail experience without the stress of big-mountain logistics.

Follow the gentle curves as the trail winds back and forth, eventually crossing paths with Big Trees Trail, Fern Ravine Trail, and finally the Wild Rose Trail. Continually stay straight to maintain the Sequoia Bayview Trail. When you reach the Sequoia Horse Arena, stay left to complete the loop in a clockwise fashion; this is the lollipop portion of your hike. Once you are roughly two-thirds of the way around the loop, find and connect with a paved road that leads back to the Sequoia Bayview Trail, concluding the loop. From there, retrace your steps to the trailhead.

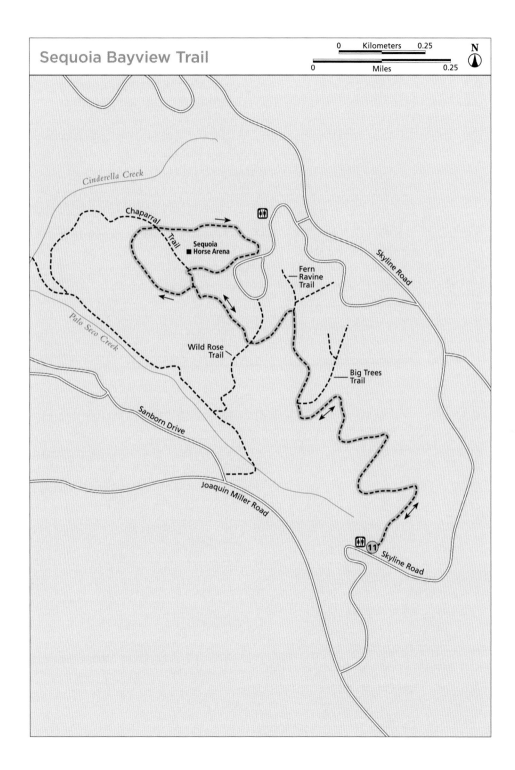

Sequoia Bayview Trail

MILES AND DIRECTIONS

0.0 Start at the trail sign at the steps across from the restroom. Turn right through the tunnel under CA 1 and bear right on the trail.

0.7 The trail intersects with Big Trees Trail to the right; stay straight.

0.8 Fern Ravine Trail bisects the trail; stay straight to stay on Sequoia Bayview Trail.

0.9 The Wild Rose Trail bisects the trail; stay straight to stay on Sequoia Bayview Trail.

1.1 You've reached the loop at the top of the trail; stay to the left to loop around the Sequoia Horse Arena.

1.5 Take a right on the paved road that runs on the south side of the horse arena.

1.7 Take a left on the Chaparral Trail that connects back to Sequoia Bayview to complete the loop.

1.8 Follow the Sequoia Bayview Trail back to the parking lot.

HILARY OLIVER

Green River Lakes to Peak Lake
Pinedale, Wyoming

Hilary Oliver is an outdoor writer, editor, and filmmaker based in Denver, Colorado. She created the blog *The Gription* (thegription.com), and is currently an editor for Outdoor Research's blog, as well as regularly contributing to *National Geographic Adventure*, *Climbing*, and *Outside*, among other publications. She first jumped into the film medium in 2016 with *Being Here*, a visual poem about the wild nature of

Hilary Oliver HILARY OLIVER

humanity. Since then, she has worked on a number of other projects including REI Co-op's *How to Run 100 Miles*, *Fall Impressions: A Yeti Tribute Story*, *High Altitude Lines: A Yeti Tribute Story*, and *Above the Fray*.

To many, the Wind River High Route is the ultimate off-trail hike in the United States, with the majority of the trek above 10,000 feet in elevation. It sticks close to the Continental Divide and has a little bit of everything stretched along its 80 miles and some 20,000 feet of elevation gain: glacial lakes, rugged traverses, panoramic views, thin air, and solitude for miles. Much of the route is off prescribed trails, so each hiker's journey may differ slightly from the next. For this reason, we've chosen to focus on the first leg of the usual 6-to-8-day route: hiking up to Peak Lake.

Nearest Town: Pinedale, Wyoming

Getting there: From Pinedale, take US 191 north for 6 miles. Then take a right on WY 352 W/Green River Lakes Road and drive for 44 miles. You will enter through the Green River Lakes campground. The trailhead is on the northeast side of the campground.

Trailhead: Green River Lakes Trailhead **GPS:** N43 23.220', W109 50.133'

Fees and Permits: None required

Trail Users: Hikers, backpackers

Elevation Gain: 3,957 feet

Length: About 40 miles RT (out-and-back)

Approximate Hiking Time: 2–4 Days

Difficulty: Strenuous

Insider Info: Peak Lake is a wonderful entry into the Wind River High Route thanks to its turquoise-colored water and stunning views of nearby Stroud Peak. With sections on- and off-trail, this portion of the Wind River High Route is an excellent trek to help you determine whether you would like to tackle the entire 80-mile distance.

Managing Agency: Bridger-Teton National Forest and Shoshone National Forest

EXPERIENCING IT

Often, the most painful trips are the most memorable.

Hilary Oliver did not grow up an outdoor enthusiast. She occasionally hiked and enjoyed being outside but she never spent a single night outdoors until she reached college. But she always carried the sentiment deep within the recesses of her mind. If she ever got the opportunity to *be* outside and spend a couple evenings under the stars, she *knew* she would fall in love.

Winning a sleeping bag in a raffle while away at school in Colorado afforded her that opportunity. New gear in hand, Hilary set about testing her limits. She spent a few nights outside—sans sleeping pad since she didn't own one—and while it was decidedly uncomfortable and a touch chilly, she didn't care. She wanted to be that person: the woman who sleeps outside with nary a care in the world while listening to the leaves rustle in the trees and feeling the grit of the dirt beneath her feet. She so badly wanted to be that person.

Throughout her 20s, she transitioned into the woman she hoped to be. She remembers thinking that all the mountains were in Colorado, showing how little of the mountainous west she had explored. But, as she grew older, she began road tripping farther and farther. She explored the Sawtooths in Idaho; the Sierra Nevada in California; the Cascades in Washington. And with every new road map and every new series

Hilary takes a break at Lake Donna, under 12,388-foot Pronghorn Peak. HILARY OLIVER

of jagged ridgelines and soaring peaks, she pieced together a bit more of her heart. Truly, the mountains were home.

It was on one of these road trips that she first remembers seeing Wyoming's Wind River Range. Her car was pointed in a southern direction toward Denver when all of a sudden a dynamic string of peaks appeared in front of her windshield, shrouded in mystery. Hilary pulled the car over and slid her atlas out from underneath the passenger seat next to her. She searched the squiggly lines and colorful striations until she identified the range on the piece of paper in her lap. This was the Wind Rivers. She didn't realize it then, but she dropped a pin in her mind to access at a later date. One day, she would walk across this range.

Years later, Hilary had grown into a different woman. She was empowered, emboldened; she possessed more self-confidence than the Hilary of her 20s. She began dating a new man—an outdoorsy fellow—and the two of them set about exploring the world. One evening, they concocted plans for the upcoming summer. After batting around a few options, the two of them zeroed in on the Wind River Range. After evaluating a few of the more popular backpacking routes—namely Cirque of the Towers and Titcomb Basin—they decided if there was ever the opportunity to go big, this was it. Hilary had once dreamed of walking across the range, so why not now? Thus, it was decided: They would complete the Wind River High Route.

Crossing a stream of runoff on the way down from Knapsack Col into Titcomb Basin
HILARY OLIVER

Hiking around Peak Lake HILARY OLIVER

Traversing off-trail was new for Hilary. They began their journey at the Green River Lakes Trailhead and enjoyed the ease of the first day as they ambled along the well-defined trail underneath hefty backpacks full of gear, food, and camera equipment. Spirits were high and outlooks positive in a manner that only happens during those initial, fresh moments of a trying journey when the exhaustion of the upcoming days has yet to settle in for the long haul. Instead, innocence and exuberance were the order of the day. They enjoyed conversation with each other, relishing the newness of their relationship amidst the magnificent scenery surrounding them.

But as day one turned into day two, the trail grew arduous and the duo left the trammeled path behind as they headed westward up toward Vista Pass. Off-route travel was tiring and Hilary struggled under the heft of her massive backpack as she crawled over large boulders and balanced her weight on loose and wobbling rocks. But she was in the epicenter of the range she had dreamt about long ago, so she ignored the ache in her back and concentrated on the task at hand. After all, she signed up for this.

Day three and day four came close to being her undoing. Travel had become strenuous and foreign; the entire route was off-trail and route-finding was beyond anything she had previously experienced. She vividly recalls standing with her boyfriend while he looked at the map, and then at the GPS, and then up at the peaks in front of them before looking back down at the map with a quizzical expression on his face. "Well," he said. "I guess we should just go up and around that big section over there. I think that will get us where we need to go."

It was largely a guessing game and they only had each other and their navigational skills to rely on. And while the physical challenge was arguably the most demanding Hilary had yet to experience in her life, the mental hurdles were equally as taxing. During one laborious day, she and her boyfriend lumbered up a steep slope filled with loose talus and massive boulders. Moving slowly, Hilary regularly lost sight of him ahead, only to catch a glimpse of him around the next bend. It was during these moments of solitude that her mind began to play tricks on her in an effort to bolster her spirits. *Camp for the night is just over this ridge, she told herself. Just make it to the top and you can stop for the day.* But that wasn't the truth and she was literally lying to herself. She crawled over the apex of the ridge, chest heaving with exertion, and looked at her boyfriend with hope radiating from her eyes. He glanced back, nonplussed, before responding: "We just need to get down there and around the corner where we can camp at the lake. Just a few more hours." Hilary was crushed. She felt unwarranted anger at him for remaining so calm and even more frustration with herself. Why had she so eagerly allowed herself to go along with her own false tales of hope?

But failure was not an option, a fact that they both well understood. Besides, this was standard. As with most backcountry adventures, her emotions wildly swung like

On the first day of the Wind River High Route, Hilary hikes from the Green River Lakes Trailhead toward Squaretop Mountain. HILARY OLIVER

PACKING TIPS FOR OFF-TRAIL TRAVEL

Few people tackle all 80 miles of the Wind River High Route, but those that do are heavily rewarded. Perhaps you'd like to attempt the traverse one day? If that's you, take a good, long look at what you pack in your backpack. Even if you are not typically an ultralight backpacker, it may be worth shedding a few ounces to make those off-trail miles easier.

- Skip the Stove. Instead, opt for cold meals that don't require any cooking. **Bonus:** You'll save on the weight of fuel, too.
- Two Pair of Socks. One can act as your hiking socks while the other can be used as your sleep socks (or emergency socks in case your feet get dunked during the day).
- Wrapped Duct Tape. Most backpackers know to bring duct tape in case of emergency, but you rarely need the entire roll. Wrap a hefty portion around your water bottle or a trekking pole to save weight.
- Homemade First Aid Kit. You don't need to buy a prepackaged kit with various pieces you'll never use. Instead, make yours at home. Not only will you save quite a few ounces, but you'll ensure you have the exact items that you need.

an out-of-control pendulum. She could swing from despair and frustration to elation and joy at the mere sight of a turquoise-colored lake. But that is the beauty of the outdoor experience; it brings out the most primal feelings in us all.

Seven days passed and Hilary and her boyfriend completed the traverse, fixing the pendulum in that state of elation. In doing so, Hilary realized she was physically capable of far more than she gave herself credit for. When she looks back on the trip now, she still recalls that single moment cresting the ridge, her heart hammering in her chest and her quads burning from the effort. She felt hollow and depleted; she was running entirely on fumes. But she kept going.

After all, if you keep doing the hardest thing you've ever done, everything else seems just a bit easier.

THE HIKE

Begin your hike at the Green River Lakes Trailhead in the Green River Lakes Recreation Area and admire the views of nearby Squaretop Mountain. From there, catch the Highline Trail/Continental Divide Trail (depending on which side of the lake you hike on, but they both end up in the same location) as it runs along the east side of Green River and churns toward the first of the Green River Lakes. This is the gentlest of introductions as the trail remains relatively flat for the first 11 miles of your journey

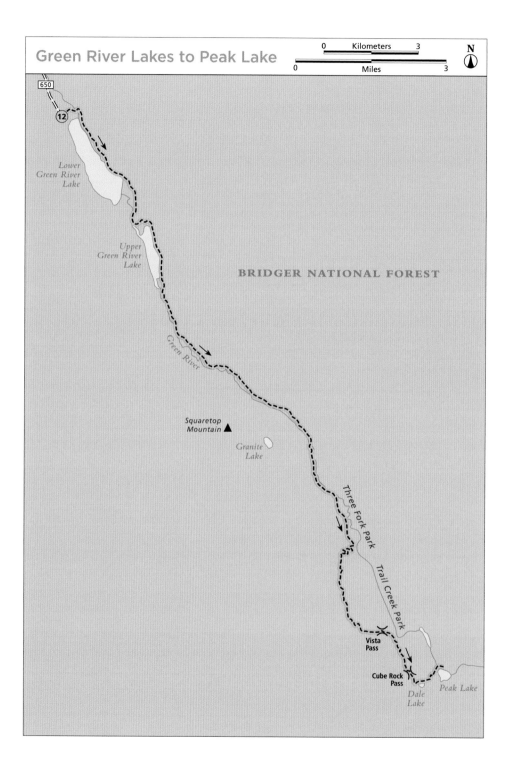

Green River Lakes to Peak Lake

0   Kilometers   3

0   Miles   3

N

650

12

Lower
Green River
Lake

Upper
Green River
Lake

BRIDGER NATIONAL FOREST

Green River

Squaretop
Mountain ▲

Granite
Lake

Three Fork Park

Trail Creek Park

Vista
Pass

Cube Rock
Pass

Dale
Lake

Peak Lake

as it wanders up the drainage of the Green River. Shortly after you pass Lower Green River Lake, you will pass Upper Green River Lake. Continue hiking beyond the two lakes and the trail will gradually climb to Three Forks Park, a beautiful open-basis area. If you are easing into this hike, Three Forks Park is an excellent (albeit popular) place to camp on the first night.

After Three Forks Park, the trail abruptly turns west and begins dramatically ascending via an off-trail route. Now you will climb to above 10,000 feet at Vista Pass. Continue on as you slightly descend before climbing back up into a boulder field to Cube Rock Pass. This portion can be very tiring and the weather finicky, so exercise caution. Thunder and lightning storms can be volatile in this area. Once you are through Cube Rock Pass, you are on the homestretch. You will soon approach Dale Lake (10,700 feet), a small body of water just to the west of Peak Lake. Shortly thereafter, you will arrive at Peak lake, your final destination. There is good camping on both the east and west sides of the lake, but even better sites can be found on the east side, so choose accordingly. ***Bonus:*** If you camp on the east side, you get a bird's-eye view of Knapsack Col, a challenging, off-trail hike that kicks off the following day for thru-hikers of the Wind River High Route.

MILES AND DIRECTIONS

0.0 Begin at the Green River Lakes Trail on the east side of the campground. You will see a wooden cabin with a trail sign to its left.

0.2 Cross the wooden bridge and reach a trail junction. Take a right for the Highline Trail.

1.5 You've reached the halfway point of Lower Green River Lake.

2.2 Trail junction; stay straight on the Highline Trail.

3.0 Trail junction; stay left on the Highline Trail. If you opted to take the trail that runs along the west side of Lower Green River Lake, this is where you will meet up with the Highline Trail.

4.1 You've reached the halfway point of Upper Green River Lake.

9.9 River crossing.

10.7 You've reached Three Forks Park.

12.4 Begin steeply climbing as the trail dramatically ascends west up some switchbacks.

13.9 You're entering the Trail Creek Park area.

15.6 The trail curves left as it heads to Vista Pass.

16.2 Vista Pass.

18.5 You've reached Cube Rock Pass on the north side of Dale Lake.

18.8 Trail junction; stay to the left to go to Peak Lake. The right trail heads to Shannon Pass.

20.0 You have arrived at Peak Lake. Turn around and return to the trailhead.

HALEY ROBISON
South Rim Trail
Marathon, Texas

Haley Robison is not only one of the youngest chief executive officers in the outdoor industry, she is also one of the few females in this top position. As CEO of outdoor

Haley Robison
ADAM SARACENO

gear company and certified benefit corporation Kammok, Haley joined the company in 2015 as chief operating officer (COO). But she quickly moved up the ranks, as she was promoted to her current position in 2016. At the helm of such an innovative outdoor brand, Haley hopes to inspire and encourage others to find their own adventures in life.

Additionally, the quarterly magazine *Conscious Company* named Haley one of the Top Conscious Business Leaders of 2018 thanks to her commitment to exemplifying conscious leadership. Over one hundred business leaders were nominated for this honor but only twenty-one were selected. Haley holds a master's degree in business administration and education from Stanford University and spent her undergraduate years at the University of Texas in Austin studying Spanish and business.

There is a place in West Texas where the nights are eerily dark and filled with sparkling stars, the coyotes howl at the moon and send goosebumps down your spine, and the Rio Grande curves around towering limestone fortresses as it gurgles along the US–Mexico border. The imposing body of water continues on its journey before emptying out into the Gulf of Mexico, preparing for its extended voyage ahead. The South Rim Trail in Big Bend National Park is one such place thanks to its stunning scenery and wilderness sentiment. It's a classically Texas hike filled with wildlife encounters (be on the lookout for cats and bears), romantic desert sunsets, colorful wildflowers, and that special mystique that can only be found in the wilds of the Lone Star State.

Nearest Town: Marathon, Texas

Getting There: From Marathon, head south on US 385 for roughly 67 miles. Take a right on Gano Springs at the Panther Junction Visitor Center and drive for approximately 3 miles. Drive 6.5 miles until you see the Chisos Basin Visitor Center. This is the trailhead.

Trailhead: Basin Trailhead **GPS:** N29 16.199', W103 18.067

Fees and Permits: $30 per vehicle or $50 annual pass to Big Bend National Park. If you opt to treat this is as a 2- or 3-day overnight hike rather than a day hike, a permit ($12) is required.

Trail Users: Hikers, backpackers, trail runners

Elevation Gain: 2,250 feet

Length: 11 miles RT (loop)

Approximate Hiking Time: 1–2 Days

Difficulty: Moderate–Strenuous

Insider Info: Most recommend doing this as a multiday hike. Not only can you better enjoy the stunning views, you can also avoid hustling through the good stuff. ***Bonus:*** Sunrise along the rim is absolutely spectacular, and the easiest way to catch it is by camping in one of the backcountry sites. The best time to hike this loop is in the winter to avoid the unbearable heat.

Managing Agency: Big Bend National Park

Marathon, Texas: The last town you drive through before reaching Big Bend GREG BALKIN

EXPERIENCING IT

According to Haley Robison, the South Rim Trail is *all Texas*. And that's just fine by her.

The 33-year-old Haley completely identifies as a Texan even though she spent the past decade bouncing around various locations like a pinball. She guided wilderness trips in Wyoming; enjoyed a National Outdoor Leadership School (NOLS) course in Utah; went to graduate school in California; studied theology in Maryland; and filled in the gaps with a consulting job that asked her to consistently travel. But after all of the excitement of constant travel wore down, Haley knew one thing: She needed to return to her roots. She needed to return to Texas.

Born in the Dallas area, Haley loves talking about her big Texas family. She sparkles when she shares stories of her outdoor childhood and laughs as she remembers cramming her homework in on the bus ride home so that she could bound up the steps, chuck her backpack inside the front door, and spend the remainder of her afternoon and evening playing outside with her friends. In quintessentially southern style, all the backyards in her neighborhood connected—no fences allowed—so Haley and her friends could wantonly frolic through the extensive ditch system, digging in the dirt and rolling in the grass until the street lights came on and she heard the dinner bell calling her home.

STARGAZING IN BIG BEND

In 2012, Big Bend National Park received gold-tier certification from the International Dark-Sky Association, effectively naming the park one of the best places in the world to stargaze. To accomplish this goal, Big Bend spent 5 years eliminating or retrofitting all the outdoor lights on the park's buildings, parking lots, and campgrounds. The result? Otherworldly beauty.

Why is Big Bend so prone to life-changing night sky views? In addition to the park's efforts to minimize the light effect, its location helps. Big Bend is relatively far away from civilization (the nearest airport is 250 miles away in Midland), minimizing potential factors that could ruin the views. While you may be able to see a few hundred stars on a clear night from any random city, you will likely witness more than 2,000 glistening stars on any given night while camped out in Big Bend. If you really want to up your chances of a memorable evening, ditch your car and hit the trail on foot. Choose a trail such as the South Rim Loop and backpack in, spending at least one night in the wilderness. Only one in ten visitors to Big Bend actually backpack in the park, so you'll have utter solitude to enjoy your unrestricted view of the Milky Way.

A beautiful view of the Pinnacles at sunset ADAM SARACENO

Texas roots are deep. They stretch far within your soul and expand around you, holding you as close as a hug and reminding you that no matter where you go or how far away you wander, you can always return. For Haley, those Texas roots constantly

Morning frost quickly melts away as the sun rises. ADAM SARACENO

tickled her heart, but it wasn't until Kammok offered her the COO position in 2015 that she finally responded to her roots. She returned to Texas; she returned home.

Kammok was the perfect fit as it is Texas to its core. Birthed in Dallas and grown in Austin, the brand encapsulates all that southern roots and Texas charm can offer. But Haley wants more than that. She wants the world to see her company—and her beloved state—as an outdoor paradise. As the second-largest state in the country, Texas has less than 2 percent of its acreage marked as public land, making this an uphill battle. States such as Oregon (53 percent) and California (46 percent) dedicate a lot more territory to public lands and, by default, the outdoor industry. But Haley won't give up because she knows Texas is something special.

Big Bend National Park encompasses over 800,000 acres of Texas territory, by far the largest swath of Texan public land and certainly the state's crown jewel of outdoor territory. Within these confines live more than 1,200 plant species, 450 bird species, 56 reptile species, and 75 mammal species. When combined with the dinosaur bones, sea fossils, and archaeological sites dating back 10,000 years, it is no wonder that Big Bend National Park is revered in its home state.

The view from the South Rim ADAM SARACENO

Looking at Mexico from the South Rim ADAM SARACENO

The South Rim Trail is easily the masterpiece of the Chisos Mountains. This hike may consist of only 11 miles, but the diversity of ecology within that short distance is memorable. Established oak and maple trees soar skyward, shading various parts of the trail, while spiky cacti and archetypal agave dot the trailside horizon. Juniper is a common sight, as is Arizona Cypress. In fact, the South Rim Trail (more specifically, the Boot Springs Trail) is the only known trail in the entirety of Big Bend to house Arizona Cypress. Once you reach the actual rim, the hike becomes less about the flora and more about the geology. Without a doubt, the view from the rim is the best viewpoint you can find. Not only can you see the iconic Rio Grande as it wraps through the park, you can also see mountains in Mexico—once your heart stops pounding from the 2,000-foot drop in front of you.

All said, the South Rim Loop is classically Texan and showcases the best of the best in terms of what the Lone Star State can offer visitors. Haley likes to compare the loop to a Salvador Dali painting with its bizarre portrayals and dynamic contrasts of space and time. It can be tough to imagine Texas coinciding with a Dalí painting, but that is why we hike: to experience the surrealism for ourselves.

THE HIKE

Although you have a few options, this description details starting up the Laguna Meadow Trail and returning via the Boot Canyon/Pinnacles Trail. Starting near the visitor center in Chisos Basin, head up the Laguna Meadow Trail until you reach a junction with the Basin Loop Trail. Follow the signs for Laguna Meadow and stay straight as you gradually climb up through multiple switchbacks, enjoying views of the saddle all the while. After roughly 1.5 miles, the climb will grow steeper and the warmup is over. Steadily climb for another 1.5 miles before hitting close to the maximum height of the trail, as well as a great place for a break.

With the steep portion behind you, gradually ascend, staying to the left at the next trail junction with Blue Creek Trail. Hike for another ½ mile, enjoying the breather as the uphill slows down, until you reach a trail junction with Colima Trail and South Rim Trail. To continue on this route, take a right and opt for the South Rim Trail. Continue on the now-level trail, eventually reaching unobstructed views of the South Rim proper. Once you hit 5.5 miles, you will have full views of the southern half of Big Bend, as well as the Santa Elena Canyon. Hike along the rim until you reach the junction with Boot Canyon Trail. To stay on this shorter route, you'll take a left and head away from the rim. Once the trail coincides with the creek bed, the scenery will dramatically change, offering towering cliffs rather than sweeping views. The trail is very straightforward from this point. Stay to the left through the first two trail junctions you encounter. Then stay right at the third junction with the Colima Trail; this will funnel you onto Pinnacles Trail, gradually descending until you hit steep switchbacks around 8.3 miles. Once you trek through these switchbacks, the remainder of the route eases downhill until you return to the trailhead at 11 miles.

MILES AND DIRECTIONS

0.0 Begin near the parking lot for Chisos Basin Visitor Center; look for the wooden sign that says "Laguna Meadows."

0.3 Stay right at the trail junction, staying on Laguna Meadow Trail.

0.7 Major trail junction with Basin Loop Trail; stay right to stay on Laguna Meadow Trail.

1.5 Steep switchbacks.

2.9 You've reached the top of the switchbacks; this is a great place to take a break.

3.1 Trail junction; stay left.

South Rim Trail

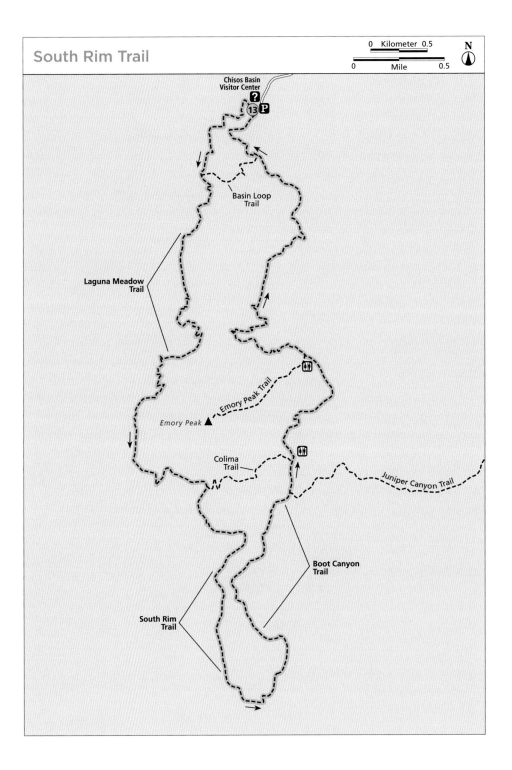

Chisos Basin
Visitor Center

13 P

Basin Loop
Trail

Laguna Meadow
Trail

Emory Peak Trail

Emory Peak ▲

Colima
Trail

Juniper Canyon Trail

Boot Canyon
Trail

South Rim
Trail

0   Kilometer 0.5

0   Mile   0.5

N

3.3 Trail junction; stay left. This location also boasts a magnificent viewpoint.

3.9 Trail junction with Colima Trail; stay right to turn onto South Rim Trail.

5.3 The best views of the South Rim, complete with a wooden sign indicating your location.

5.8 More excellent views of the South Rim.

5.9 Trail junction; stay left to hike onto Boot Canyon Trail.

7.1 Trail junction with Juniper Canyon Trail; stay left.

7.3 Trail junction with Colima Trail; stay to the right.

8.0 Best views of a prominent rock spire to the east.

8.3 Trail junction with Emory Peak Trail; stay to the right (unless you opt to summit Emory Peak).

8.4 Steep downhill switchbacks.

10.2 You will see a resting bench if you need it, but you are almost finished!

10.6 Trail junction; stay right.

11.0 Arrive back at your car.

ELYSE RYLANDER
Shoup Bay Trail – Section A
Valdez, Alaska

Elyse Rylander is an outdoor guide and instructor, as well as the founder of OUT There Adventures (OTA), a nonprofit designed to empower queer young adults through a personal relationship with the outdoors. Her work has appeared in places like the *Routledge International Handbook of Outdoor Studies* as well as various speaking panels. In March, 2018, Elyse was named a Top Woman in Conservation and Environmental Justice by *ECODiversity Magazine*. Additionally, she is the co-organizer of the LGBTQ Outdoor Summit, an annual event dedicated to cultivating connections and building community in an effort to encourage more inclusivity for LGBTQ peers in the outdoor industry.

Elyse Rylander CLAYTON BOYD PHOTOGRAPHY

The Shoup Bay Trail is a sampler platter of everything you would want in an Alaskan hiking adventure. Wilderness, scenery, wildlife, glistening bays, solitude—the list goes on and on. Its proximity to Valdez makes it an easily accessible trail for anyone. But the lack of maintenance (see sidebar) poses extreme adventure on a good day and downright frustration on a bad day. Be sure to communicate with locals or the Valdez Adventure Alliance before hitting the trail to make sure you are well informed of its current conditions. This guide focuses on the first half (Section A) since it is more reliably maintained.

Nearest Town: Valdez, Alaska

Getting There: If you are already in Valdez, you are practically at the trailhead. Make your way to the far west end of Egan Drive. You will see a parking area on the left side; this is the trailhead.

Trailhead: Shoup Bay Trailhead **GPS:** N61 08.162', W146 23.427

Fees and Permits: None required

Trail Users: Hikers, backpackers, trail runners

Elevation Gain: 850 feet

Length: 6.8 miles RT (out-and-back)

Approximate Hiking Time: Half Day–Full Day

Difficulty: Moderate

Insider Info: Shoup Bay Trail–Section A is the first segment of the full Shoup Bay Trail. For the full 20-mile roundtrip hike, tack on the second segment, called Section B. Depending on the season, budget, and land management, the trail may or may not be overgrown and difficult to locate past Section A.

Managing Agency: Shoup Bay State Marine Park with Valdez Adventure Alliance

EXPERIENCING IT

Elyse Rylander (she/her) was only 4 weeks old when her parents took her on their first family canoe trip down the Wisconsin River. Four weeks is a daunting age for any new parents, let alone ones embarking on a float trip, but being outside was ingrained in her family. It was who they were; it was what they did. That family tradition continued for almost every summer of Elyse's childhood.

Born and raised in southern Wisconsin in a small town of 2,000 people, Elyse came from a family with modest means. Her mother was a teacher and her father a carpenter, so they did well enough but certainly weren't overloaded with cash. But her parents decidedly believed in the healing and rejuvenating powers of fresh air, so they took the family on outdoor adventures as often as time and finances would allow. They canoed the Wisconsin River every weekend possible and if they weren't canoeing, they spent the summer evenings in a tent on a car-camping excursion. Winter brought frigid weather and never-ending snow drifts to this northerly state, so the family transitioned from sleeping in a tent to sliding down hills on skis. Being outside was a year-round endeavor that did not end when they returned home.

Soaking in the view of Shoup Bay MATT YORK

Their family house sat on 12 acres of pristine playground. Elyse and her sister were the best of friends, spending every waking moment running around outside and only coming in to sleep and eat. They would go to school the next day, fulfill their obligations, and then head back outside and repeat the entire process once more. If there was ever a life lived outdoors, this was as close as it got.

As she grew older, the outdoor space became less of a carefree romper room and more of a mindful respite for Elyse. She learned more about herself through introspection and realized that her family did not share the same conservative values as many others in their small Wisconsin community. As a result, Elyse was frequently the target of bullying. This sporadically continued throughout her teen and young adult years, acting as an intermittent yet regular source of aggravation. To combat the emotions that bubbled to the surface after these encounters, Elyse would head outside with her running shoes or grab a paddle and hit the river. These outdoor endeavors challenged and excited her, always presenting new and different obstacles for her to overcome. As a result, she grew emboldened and confident, knowing that she possessed skill sets that many of her peers did not. She felt unique and special.

Wanting to continue those feelings of acceptance, at 16 Elyse accepted a job at Rutabaga Paddlesports, a specialty paddle retailer located in nearby Madison. She still felt the most at ease while outside, so she figured the next logical step would be to work in that same environment. Rutabaga offered a special summer training program for high school students who wanted to be paddling instructors. Elyse completed the program, cementing her job as a paddling instructor for the remainder of her high school years.

Shoup Bay under blue skies REESE DOYLE

More emphatic, however, were the relationships Elyse formed during her time at Rutabaga. She recently came to terms with her own identity and was dating her first girlfriend, but she had never met or known an openly queer woman. This changed when she met Mo Kappes, her boss at Rutabaga. Mo challenged everything Elyse thought she had known and empowered Elyse to be true to herself. Mo was bigger than life and everything Elyse wanted from herself and from her future. In watching Mo in her daily routine, Elyse knew one thing: She wanted to do this for the rest of her life. She wanted to help other people find the same acceptance and connections she had found through the power of the outdoors.

It was not until years later (in 2014) that the nonprofit OUT There Adventures was legally founded, but it was emotionally created on that day 12 years ago when Elyse met Mo. But first, Elyse was not done adventuring. Before OTA, there was Alaska.

While in college, Elyse continued to pursue her love for Mother Nature by spending her summers as a commercial guide in the Prince William Sound of Alaska. At the time, she was studying communications, a degree that was not remotely interesting to her. She was mentally dabbling with the idea of founding her own program, but nothing had concretely solidified in her mind. So instead, she ventured north to spend her days paddling on the brisk and clear bays that magically appeared around the perimeter of the Prince William Sound.

While guiding, Elyse lived in Valdez, a mere two-minute walk from the Shoup Bay Trailhead. With such unfettered access, she found herself consistently returning to the bayside trail. On most days, she opted to lace up her running shoes and complete the first segment to Gold Creek and back, soaking in the scenic views of the water from a very different angle than she was accustomed to seeing while guiding on the boats. If she awoke with a little extra kick in her step, she would opt for the full-scale adventure, journeying

Shoup Bay and Shoup Glacier as seen from the saddle halfway along the trail REESE DOYLE

LACK OF FUNDING IS CRUSHING ALASKA'S TRAIL SYSTEMS

If you traveled to Valdez a few years ago to hike this route, there is a great chance that you would have noticed an integral component missing: the trail. While Alaska is the biggest state in the country, with the largest state park system (3.6 million acres) to match, its budget is tiny by comparison. For example, the park system received $14 million in 2017, which is laughable when compared to California's $522 million in the same year.

As a result, many trails have slipped into disrepair thanks to deferred maintenance, and the Shoup Bay Trail is one of them. In 2015, Alaska announced they were searching for permittees to run three of the Valdez-area parks and trails, including the Shoup Bay area. A nonprofit called Valdez Adventure Alliance (VAA) answered the call, knowing that it would be devastating to Valdez's tourism economy to close the trails. It took their team 3 weeks to clear a 7-mile stretch of trail during the summer of 2017 thanks to the subarctic rainforest that grows insanely fast in that season.

But the future is still unclear. Without state funds, VAA quickly realized that the income from the huts and camping fees at the campground weren't enough to fund the maintenance. Locals chipped in, as did a few Valdez-based restaurants, and VAA even received a grant from the Department of Transportation. But it is a sketchy arrangement at best and if the summer of 2018 is any indication, the trail is still a choose-your-own adventure of sorts.

the entire length of the trail, all the way down to Shoup Bay proper. Inevitably, these days called for lengthy hours of bushwhacking and a general interest in Type-II fun, both familiar concepts to her outdoor-loving soul.

The exploration of the trail didn't stop when she kicked off her shoes. Still a paddler at heart, Elyse regularly powered herself from Valdez to Shoup Bay and back again via the helm of a kayak. She frequently took clients out on the bay, but she also enjoyed the voyage for its calm, solo moments. Truly, it didn't matter if it was via land or sea; Shoup Bay became her happy place during her four years in Alaska.

It was in these periods of solitude that Elyse encountered her near-religious experiences that validated her career path in the outdoors. Not being someone who grew up with religion, Elyse still recalls one memorable visit to the bay that reinforced her life choices. She trekked into the lower bay area, envisioning the schools of salmon that frequented the zone. Because of the fish, eagles prefer the area as well. As she trekked down the rolling hill, she saw dozens of eagles' nests dotting the skyline, perching high in the trees as if protectively guarding their community. A handful of eagles soared through the sky, their majestic wings floating on the breeze as they coasted in circles against the filtered rays of sunshine that drifted down onto their lightly warmed feathers. The glacier served as a backdrop to this seemingly fictitious scenario, and Elyse found herself feeling content with her plan. She was okay; everything would be okay. After all, eagles never lie.

The last summer she spent in Alaska was the launching summer for OUT There Adventures (OTA). These days, OTA accomplishes exactly what Elyse had hoped it would all those years ago, although it looks nothing like she originally planned. Originally slated to be a "gay Outward Bound," she quickly realized after the first season that the participants needed and wanted more than just a general outdoor experience. In fact, of the 300 Seattle youth she met with during the first summer, only 2 people showed up for the actual trip. Albeit accidentally, OTA had stumbled upon the elephant in the room: the major disconnect between the community they were trying to serve and the experiences they were offering.

Since then, OTA has blended the outdoor experiential focus with community outreach in an effort to tackle the systemic barriers that prevent those excited classroom students from actually signing up for a course once the bell rings. It is exhausting and challenging work, and some days Elyse feels like she is merely chipping away at the barriers rather than crushing them. But it is forward progress all the same and she is grateful to do it.

But that does not mean that troublesome days don't leave her feeling depleted and fatigued, so filled with the weighted sense of her goals that it is akin to walking through sludge. When these days do happen, Elyse simply needs to think back to her eagles in Shoup Bay. After all, the eagles have shown her that everything will be okay.

It's easy to see why the trail grows wild—everything is so lush and green! MATT YORK

Shoup Bay Trail-Section A

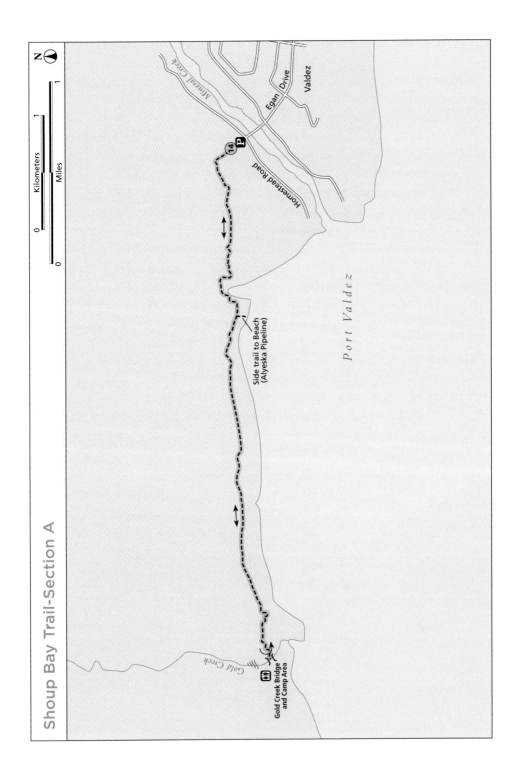

N

Kilometers
0   1

Miles
0   1

Mineral Creek

Egan Drive

Valdez

Homestead Road

14
P

Side trail to Beach
(Alyeska Pipeline)

Port Valdez

Gold Creek

Gold Creek Bridge
and Camp Area

THE HIKE

Starting from the parking area at the west end of Egan Drive, hike along the flat, 4-foot-wide trail as it wraps through lowlands. Some areas are very muddy and damp, so long pants are advised. In less than 1 mile the trail leaves behind the dense alder forest and opens up into grasslands with a spotty boardwalk. This is used to prevent flooding during exceptionally wet conditions. Continue hiking, passing a small spur trail to your left. This goes to the beach, which affords views of the Alyeska Pipeline, if that is something you find interesting. If you would rather continue on, climb up the steep hillside. Near the summit, you will cross two small streams that can be tricky in rainy conditions, so exercise caution. This pinnacle also offers sweeping views of Valdez to the east and Port Valdez to the south and west. Take a moment to enjoy your viewpoint before continuing on.

From the high point, steeply descend to the Gold Creek Bridge and camping area, where you will find restrooms and bear-proof containers. The Gold Creek Bridge marks the turnaround point for Section A, but note that this bridge can be tricky to get to in rough conditions as Gold Creek frequently floods. Return to the trailhead on the same route.

MILES AND DIRECTIONS

0.0 Begin at the parking lot on the far west end of Egan Drive in Valdez.

0.8 Leave the alder forest and enter the open grassland section of the trail.

1.1 A spur trail shoots to the left to a viewpoint of Alyeska Pipeline Terminal. Stay straight to continue on the Shoup Bay Trail.

1.5 The trail begins to ascend the hillside.

2.3 Cross first small stream.

2.7 Enjoy the stunning views of Port Valdez and the town of Valdez.

2.8 Begin descending hillside.

3.1 Trail junction; the spur to the left leads to Gold Creek camping area. Stay straight to find the bridge.

3.4 You've reached Gold Creek Bridge. This is the turnaround point. Follow the trail back to the parking lot.

SHAWNTÉ SALABERT
Campo to Warner Springs
Campo, California

Shawnté Salabert is a writer in the outdoor industry who prefers to write about the land, the people, and the connection between the two. Based in Los Angeles, she has ample opportunities to observe humans of all varieties, but her passion for the outdoors affords her the opportunity to experience the former. Her writing has appeared in *Outside*, *Backpacker Magazine*, *Alpinist*, and *Adventure Journal*, among others. Her book, *Hiking the Pacific Crest Trail: Southern California*, hit stands in December 2017.

Shawnté Salabert KAM ALTAR

To many, the first 100 miles of the Pacific Crest Trail is viewed as a desert slog that must be completed to get to "the good stuff." This sentiment couldn't be any further from the truth, a fact that surprises many. As the gateway to the Laguna Mountains, the trail is more verdant and rolling than most hikers expect. Be prepared for long stretches without any water and gusty winds, but also magnificent sunsets and a romantic western beauty.

Nearest Town: Campo, California

Getting There: From San Diego, take CA 94 E for 5 miles before hooking up with CA 125 N. Drive 2 miles before taking exit #18A to merge onto I-8 E. Stay on I-8 E for 36 miles before taking exit #51 for Buckman Springs Road. Take a right and drive 10 miles. Then take another right on CA 94 W. Drive 1.5 miles, then take a left and a slight right at Railway Museum Road. Drive 1.4 miles, take a left, and you will be at the official beginning to the Pacific Crest Trail. While you can't park at the beginning (as that would seriously offend and concern the US Border Patrol), you can park nearby in Campo.

Trailhead: Pacific Crest Trail Trailhead **GPS:** N32 35.383', W116 28.018'

Fees and Permits: The Pacific Crest Trail Association does not issue permits for segments of travel less than 500 miles. That said, you may need to obtain a permit for various wilderness areas you intend to camp in, so do your research ahead of time.

Trail Users: Hikers, backpackers, trail runners

Elevation Gain: 16,205 feet

Length: 104 miles (point-to-point)

Approximate Hiking Time: 1–2 Weeks

Difficulty: Strenuous

Insider Info: This hike is the first section of the famous Pacific Crest Trail that spans the length of the country from Mexico to Canada. While Section A is largely believed to be desert, this segment will surprise you with its beauty and often steep climbs. Be prepared for anything, plan your food and water accordingly, and leave a little trail magic behind for any thru-hikers you meet along the way.

Managing Agency: Pacific Crest Trail Association

Enjoying the desert drama in Anza-Borrego Desert State Park SHAWNTÉ SALABERT

EXPERIENCING IT

Shawnté Salabert is arguably one of the most sought-after freelance writers in the outdoor industry. But if you ask her how she arrived at her current situation as one of the most well-respected and educated sources of information on the Southern and Central California sections of the Pacific Crest Trail, she will laugh and tell you a story about the Boys and Girls Club of America.

Shawnté grew up on the south side of Milwaukee in a self-described low-income neighborhood. With a young single mother who constantly worked, Shawnté learned to entertain herself at a young age. From the front door of their home, there were three buildings within walking distance: a crack house to the left, a bar to the right, and the local Boys and Girls Club in the middle. Fortunately, the Boys and Girls Club became Shawnté's refuge of sorts, and she spent as much of her free time in that building as she possibly could. She popped in after school and whiled away the afternoons chatting with the staff; she swung by on weekends when her mom was at work and hung out with anyone who happened to be in the building. She grew to know and understand the various staff members, and in turn, they learned a lot about her. Over time, they formed unbreakable bonds that Shawnté still recalls fondly.

When she was 8 years old, one of the staff members approached Shawnté about attending summer camp for a single night. Since her mother didn't own a car and they either walked or took the bus everywhere, the notion of getting out of the city was beyond thrilling. She agreed and was quickly whisked away to Camp Whitcomb/Mason in Hartland, Wisconsin, a town roughly 30 miles west of Milwaukee.

For Shawnté, Camp Whitcomb/Mason was the place of her dreams. The smell of warmed sap wafted through camp from the large pine forest, enticing her with earthy smells she never before experienced in the city. The lush green meadow was a revelation, beckoning to her with its soft and thick surface, inviting camp kids to lay down and stay awhile. The crystal-blue lake sparkled and glimmered in the sunshine, reflecting excitement and joy while affording the campers a brisk yet invigorating dip beneath the undulating surface of its water. And the cabins! Small, cozy cabins dotted the ethereal landscape, each housing the cool college kids that Shawnté wished were her own brothers and sisters.

She only spent one night at camp but she was immediately smitten. Not only did she fall in love with the camp itself, but this single 24-hour experience ignited a passion for the great outdoors. Shawnté returned to Milwaukee and immediately told her mom that she wanted to go back to camp as frequently as possible.

And so it went. Subsequent summers saw Shawnté out in Hartland at Camp Whitcomb/Mason. Her mom couldn't afford a dime of the attendance fees, but somehow, the staff at the Boys and Girls Club always managed to find a way for Shawnté to attend. They granted her scholarships or came up with systems that allowed her to visit camp for a nominal $15 fee. Many times, her Boys and Girls Club counselors scraped together the cash from their personal bank accounts and paid her camp

THE HISTORY OF THE PACIFIC CREST TRAIL

The Pacific Crest Trail (PCT) is a 2,659-mile trail that stretches from the US–Mexico border in California all the way up to the US–Canada border in Washington. Along with the Appalachian Trail and the Continental Divide Trail, the PCT is the third trail that completes the Triple Crown of Hiking.

First proposed in 1932 by Clinton C. Clarke, the "father of the PCT," the original proposal was to link up the John Muir Trail, the Tahoe-Yosemite Trail, the Skyline Trail, and the Cascade Crest Trail. Exploration began and the first meeting of the Pacific Crest Trail System Conference took place in 1935, with the trail first appearing on a government map in 1939. But the onset of World War II brought a halt to the trail building, which wasn't resumed for a decade. The PCT was finally named a National Scenic Trail in 1968 with the first guidebook coming five years later in 1973. The U.S. Forest Service hired its first full-time PCT program manager in 2000, a strong indicator of the growth of the trail.

Climbing toward the shoulder of Morena Butte SHAWNTÉ SALABERT

tuition themselves. They knew it was her favorite place on the planet and she deserved to be there, so they found ways to make it happen.

A pastoral walk near Warner Springs SHAWNTÉ SALABERT

For Shawnté, those camp summers were a revelation. She wore her favorite outfit every day—a kitty-cat shirt and Milwaukee Brewers shorts with piping on the side—because she wanted to show her best self at her best place. She learned to fish, eagerly dangling the line into the glimmering water, anticipating that familiar tug on the end. She learned to swim and play capture the flag; she rowed a canoe and practiced sign language with her new friends. And she *had* friends, a fact that Shawnté found both intimidating and thrilling all at once. Camp afforded her mental peace and rest, both emotions that were tough to come across back at home.

When she grew too old to be a camper and too young to be on staff, Shawnté volunteered her time, knowing that it was still where she wanted to be more than anywhere else. Then she became a counselor, teaching environmental education and arts and crafts. As the years blew by, Shawnté aged, thinking that she would graduate high school and become a full-time camp counselor. That was her life's goal.

But then, the dream grew bigger and grander. Knowing that her mother couldn't pay one cent of any college tuition, Shawnté was awarded a full-ride scholarship to the University of Wisconsin–Stevens Point thanks to the Boys and Girls Club. She studied history and sociology, eventually earning herself a graduate degree in social work. For a while, it seemed as if her plan to work in the outdoors had been forgotten, but life had a funny way of coming full circle.

For a decade, Shawnté bounced. She moved from Wisconsin to South Carolina, and then to New York. She worked in social work before realizing it was too stressful and transitioned into the art scene. Then her employer lost funding and cut her job. There she was, at the dead of winter in New York City, with no job, no money, and not a lot of heat. Things were looking dire when she ran into an old photographer

A hiker descends to Barrel Springs. SHAWNTÉ SALABERT

friend who invited her to Los Angeles. Knowing her options were limited and eager for year-round warmth, she threw caution to the wind, packed up her belongings, and began her voyage west.

Twelve years later and Shawnté never looked back. Upon her arrival in California's epicenter, she began writing for Modern Hiker, one of the largest hiking websites in the country. Feeling out of place and lost with her career trajectory, Shawnté questioned her abilities as a writer and doubted her competency. But Modern Hiker was growing and needed fresh blood. Shawnté jumped in with two feet, enjoying the feel of the pen once again while reveling in writing about her childhood favorite: the outdoors.

Unbeknownst to Shawnté, a publishing company approached the founder of Modern Hiker, looking for an author to write a guidebook for the Pacific Crest Trail. Without the bandwidth, he passed on the opportunity but threw one name into the talent pool of potential authors: Shawnté Salabert.

She remembers it like it was yesterday. It was 6 months later, and she was sitting at home when an email popped into her inbox from a publishing company, asking if she would be interested in writing a book on the Pacific Crest Trail. Having no knowledge that her résumé had already been researched and fielded, Shawnté believed the email to be a joke and quite literally went to press delete. But then something stopped her. What if this was real? Was there any harm in responding? She weighed her options

Lake Morena comes into view. SHAWNTÉ SALABERT

and realized it never hurts to try. She shot an email back, expressing her interest in the potential project.

It was an email that changed the course of her life. It changed everything.

Eventually contracted to write the book, Shawnté spent the next two years hiking every single mile of the Pacific Crest Trail as it wound through Southern California. She became an expert on her 1,000-mile stretch, hiking it over and over again with every spare moment of her time. She soon took a 2-month sabbatical from work, opting to devote all of her time, energy, and resources to research for her project. She believed she was on the path—*her* path—but it never became so clear as on one single night she spent in the High Sierra. It was late but she couldn't sleep. Instead, she posted up outside of her tent, admiring the dazzling stars radiating throughout the night sky. While watching Mother Nature's ultimate light show, she felt the epiphany hit her as hard as a black bear running through camp: If there was ever going to be a good time to take her dream and run with it, this was it. This was her moment. This was her time to grasp her dreams and grow them into her reality. It wasn't an easy

Shawnté rides high on Eagle Rock. SHAWNTÉ SALABERT

decision since her background taught her to never take financial risks—and certainly never quit your job—but she knew it was right. She went for it.

Four years later, Shawnté is living the life she dreamt of as a little girl back in the Boys and Girls Club. Her book on the Southern and Central California sections of the Pacific Crest Trail was published in December 2017, and she has since filled her calendar with writing assignments for various nationally recognized outdoor publications. She travels. She collaborates with her personal heroes. She speaks at public events. She participates in backpacking courses for future or potential thru-hikers. She hosts presentations around her book.

She lives her dream.

THE HIKE

I realize that you likely won't be using only this book if you intend to hike the first 104 miles of the Pacific Crest Trail. Or at least I hope that isn't the case. That said, this is meant to give you a general description of the hike so that you can better research and prepare yourself should you decide to tackle this beautiful yet exhausting first leg of the trail.

Begin at the southern terminus, a series of pillars located on the US–Mexico border. Your elevation here is 2,915 feet above sea level. Let the emotions wash over you because you won't be done hiking until you are more than 100 miles to the north.

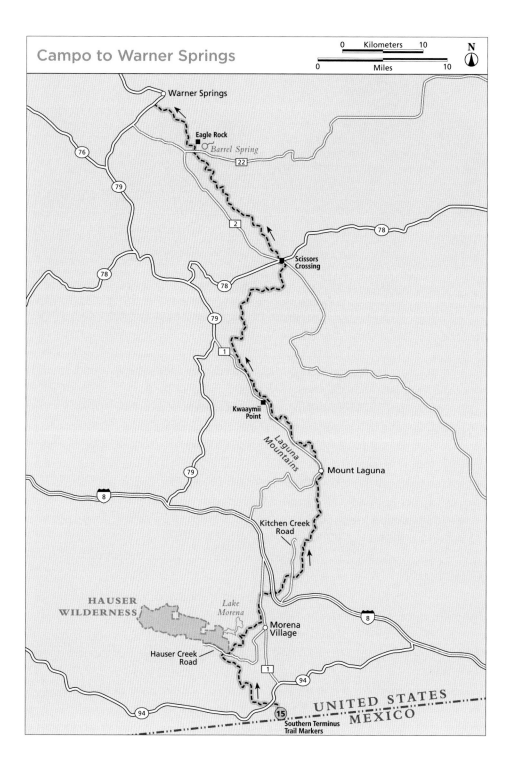

Campo to Warner Springs

0   Kilometers   10
0   Miles   10

N

Warner Springs

Eagle Rock
76   Barrel Spring
79   22
2
78
Scissors
Crossing
78
78
79
1
Kwaaymii
Point
Laguna
Mountains
Mount Laguna
79
8
Kitchen Creek
Road
HAUSER   Lake
WILDERNESS   Morena
Morena
Village   8
Hauser Creek
Road   1
94
94   UNITED STATES
15   MEXICO
Southern Terminus
Trail Markers

Of that 100 miles, the first three-quarters of the trail follow the Laguna Mountains, a range east of San Diego that houses plenty of grasslands. The rolling trail drops in and out of Hauser Canyon and continues northbound as it passes Lake Morena. Once you pass the lake, you will begin climbing out of the Morena Valley; this is your first stretch of serious climbing. You will eventually top out just above 6,000 feet in elevation, eventually summiting and passing through the small, aptly named town of Mount Laguna. Then continue along the Laguna Mountain Plateau Rim and cross your fingers that you catch hang gliders at the ever-popular Kwaaymii Point. From there, you will soon reach the Rodriquez Spur water tank. This is where you leave the Laguna Mountains.

Hike down into the San Felipe Valley, eventually reaching the Scissors Crossing in Anza Borrego, where two roads scissor-cross each other. From here many opt for a long day to cover the 22 miles into Barrel Spring. This stretch makes it easy with beautiful cacti and succulents covering the landscape the entire time, reminding you of the dry-loving plant life that you will eventually leave behind. Then, from Barrel Spring, wander through a few meadows and pass by Eagle Rock, an aptly named formation that looks very obviously like an eagle. Continue hiking as the trail then dumps you into Warner Springs, the official end of Section A of the Pacific Crest Trail.

MILES AND DIRECTIONS

0.0 Begin at the southern terminus near the trail markers. You are at Mile 0.

12.9 Trail crosses into Hauser Wilderness.

18.1 You are near the eastern shores of Lake Morena.

20.0 You've reached the Lake Morena Campground, home of the former PCT kickoff party.

25.0 The Pacific Crest Trail crosses over the top of the old I-8 and underneath the new I-8.

26.0 The trail now begins climbing in earnest as you hike 3,000 feet up into the Laguna Mountains.

30.0 Cross Kitchen Creek Road.

39.2 The small town of Mount Laguna is at just over 6,000 feet.

52.0 Kwaaymii Point.

68.4 Rodriquez Spur water tank.

77.0 You've reached Scissors Crossing.

99.0 You've reached Barrel Spring.

101.1 Poke around in the formations; you should be able to find Eagle Rock.

104.0 Welcome to Warner Springs.

AMBREEN TARIQ
Western Ridge Trail
Silver Spring, Maryland

Ambreen Tariq is the founder of the Instagram platform @BrownPeopleCamping, which she launched in 2016 to celebrate the National Park Service's centennial. As a Muslim, South-Asian female immigrant, Ambreen uses her personal life experiences via this social media initiative to discuss the role of privilege in the outdoor space. Additionally, she hopes to promote and encourage a love of the outdoors for everyone, regardless of his or her ability, background, or experience. By day, Ambreen is a nonpracticing attorney who works for the federal government in Washington, DC. She is an ambassador for Merrell and Airstream, while also holding voluntary board member positions with the City Kids Wilderness Project and Green Muslims.

Ambreen Tariq AMBREEN TARIQ

Located smack in the middle of the hustle and bustle of Washington, DC, this under-the-radar gem avoids the crowds in popular Rock Creek Park. The undulating terrain of this out-and-back is like a roller coaster ride, taking you up and down the ridges to catch a glimpse of beautiful views. While you can still see roads or buildings from most of the hike, this is a quiet and peaceful trail to hit up when you just need to get out of the city's madness.

Nearest Town: Silver Spring, Maryland

Getting There: Head east on I-410. Take a right on Beach Drive; drive 1.1 miles and you will see a parking lot off Beach Drive on the left, right at the Washington, DC and Maryland border.

Trailhead: Boundary Bridge **GPS:** N38 59.191', W77 03.139'

Fees and Permits: None

Trail users: Hikers, trail runners, mountain bikers, and equestrians

Elevation Gain: 460 feet

Length: 9 miles (point-to-point)

Approximate Hiking Time: Half Day

Difficulty: Moderate

Insider Info: The creek is at its highest in late spring and early summer, so that is a good time to visit for photos of the water. However, autumn is particularly scenic thanks to fall foliage.

Managing Agency: National Park Service

EXPERIENCING IT

It was a cold January day when Ambreen Tariq first set foot on American soil. Snow piled high on the sides of the road, but it wasn't the fluffy stuff of Christmas lore. Instead, the lumpy piles were dark and brown from the hardships of car exhaust and repetitive foot traffic, dreary indicators that the long days of Minnesota winters had settled in for the duration. Just shy of 8 years old, Ambreen hadn't expected such a frosty American reception, but she was willing to wait it out. After all, America was the land of plenty and she was exhilarated to explore her new country.

Time passed as it is wont to do, and Ambreen's parents continued to bust their butts to provide limitless opportunities for their two daughters. One day, her father came home from work bustling with enthusiasm; he had some news to share. They were going on a family camping trip! The concept of beautiful, clean, and free outdoor spaces was new to this Indian family, but everyone was up for the challenge. Her

Fall is a beautiful season to hike this trail. AMBREEN TARIQ

parents scraped together enough money to buy the basics like a tent and sleeping bags before packing up the car and hitting the road.

This excursion was the first of many as the family grew to love their camping road trips around the state. Not only were they an opportunity to explore their new home, they also became Ambreen's escape from her realities as an immigrant child. At school, she struggled to adjust to her surroundings. Her darker skin tone and exotic lunch food were fodder for the playground bullies who didn't understand that cultural differences were to be celebrated, not feared. She was just a kid, but she sensed that she was unique in her classroom, and she didn't know what that meant. It was a confusing time for Ambreen.

However, Mother Nature is frequently a great equalizer, so Ambreen found comfort and solace in being outside. She learned to build a campfire and played with bugs while laughing and enjoying traditional Indian food for dinner. She now acknowledges that her family's outdoor experiences were limited, but that didn't matter: They opened up a new world of possibility.

A dense canopy shades the trail from full sun. Ambreen Tariq

Even so, Ambreen couldn't help but notice that her outdoor experiences reflected what she learned at school. It was easy to see that her family didn't look like the other families at the campground, and while everyone was polite, no one ever swung by the

Tariq's campsite for a fireside chat. They kept to themselves and so did Ambreen and her family.

The years rolled by and Ambreen's love for the outdoors grew. She went on to bigger and more elaborate backpacking trips, always thankful that she could afford the airfare or gear needed for such an expensive endeavor. But, even as she continued to love hiking decades later, she noticed the same thing: A lack of diversity on the trails. So frequently, she would be the only brown-skinned woman out there, a fact that she still chalks up to a lack of accessibility and authenticity. Not everyone can dive neck-deep into the world of peak bagging and multiday backpacking trips; it simply isn't realistic for everyone. However, Ambreen believes strongly that anything out your door can be considered "the outdoors" and hopes that everyone—regardless of skin tone—will find the opportunity to explore just a bit of Mother Nature. For this reason, she fell in love with the Western Ridge Trail.

Located in Washington, DC's Rock Creek Park, the Western Ridge Trail embodies the heart of the human experience. The park itself splits through the middle of the city, a welcome green space in a sea of concrete and automobiles, lobbyists and politicians. Interestingly, Rock Creek was once an honest-to-goodness national park as we now know them, bound within the confines of a booming metropolis. Created by an act of Congress in 1890, it was the third national park; only Yellowstone National Park (1872) and Mackinac National Park (1875; now Mackinac Island State Park)

Sunlight filters down beneath the canopy. AMBREEN TARIQ

The crunch of the leaves fills the air with the sounds of fall. AMBREEN TARIQ

preceded it. However, if you check the list of sixty national parks, you will notice Rock Creek isn't listed between Redwood and Rocky Mountain National Park. And that's because it isn't on the list.

POPULAR ATTRACTIONS

In addition to the 32 miles of hiking trails, Rock Creek Park boasts a wide array of cultural and historical attractions to visit. For starters, the Rock Creek Park Nature Center houses the only planetarium in the entire National Park Service. Along with monthly stargazing sessions, high-tech Spitz software projects starry images of the night sky onto a dome-shaped ceiling. Or, if you're a history buff, check out Peirce Mill. Built in the 1820s, it remained in operation until 1897, although it no longer functions today. The Old Stone House is another aptly named attraction for those wanting a glimpse into our past. Constructed in the eighteenth century, this humble stone home stands mighty amidst the high-powered and ostentatious buildings found in the rest of the city. While it once housed a clock shop, today it commemorates the ordinary Americans who built this nation from its early days.

The stream roars by during a
warm summer day. AMBREEN TARIQ

In 1933, the title of the parklands in the District of Columbia was transferred to the National Park Service, thus creating what was then called the National Capital Parks. This didn't last long as the name was changed back to National Park Service in 1935. However, despite a recent push to include the word "national" in the name, Rock Creek Park is currently listed as an "other designation" under the umbrella of the Park Service. Because of this, Rock Creek Park is an oft-overlooked gem that doesn't necessarily get the wilderness cred it so seriously deserves.

For its part, the Western Ridge Trail epitomizes the two factors Ambreen finds essential to inclusion in the outdoors: accessibility and authenticity. Thanks to its location on the west side of the park, this rolling trail is easy to find, and hikers can hop on and off as they see fit, making it attainable to anyone in the city, regardless of whether or not they own a vehicle. In fact, it's probably better if you don't have a car (as most don't in the city); catch the metro and you can easily find yourself at the trailhead. It even swings by various picnic areas, as well as the Nature Center and Planetarium, so those dabbling in hiking or hoping for a nice, mellow day will have bonus attractions.

But most importantly, the Western Ridge Trail doesn't try to be anything that it's not. This isn't a lung-busting, middle-of-nowhere, extreme hiking junkies–only type of trail. Rather, it's made for everyone, including those who may discount their outdoor prowess. This is why it takes the top spot on Ambreen's list. She understands how many of her peers designate the outdoors as that thing over there: something that is either unattainable or, at minimum, a laborious undertaking. The Western Ridge Trail is neither of those things and instead acts as a unifying track that invites anyone from any background to explore its gentle curves. And that's why it is special to Ambreen.

THE HIKE

From the parking lot, walk back to Beach Drive and look across the road; you will see the trailhead for your hike. Cross the street and catch the trail by the sign that says, "Welcome to Rock Creek Park." Almost immediately, the hike starts off on a moderate uphill as the trail climbs away from Rock Creek. There is a thick tree canopy so this part of the hike is shady. You soon cross Wise Road; continue on the path on the other side of the street. Hike downhill, eventually reaching an unmarked intersection; stay straight to maintain Western Ridge Trail. Around this time, you will also begin noticing green blazes on these trees. Follow these for the remainder of your hike as these indicate the Western Ridge Trail. Cross Pinehurst Branch by walking across the river on stepping stones before reaching a marked four-way intersection with Pinehurst Branch Trail. Once again, stay straight to stay on Western Ridge.

From here until Bingham Drive it gets confusing, as there are multiple unmarked trails that are not delineated on the map. About ¼ mile after the Pinehurst Branch Trail intersection, you will see a stake with two green blazes, the top one angled to the right. This indicates you should take the right trail. Stay straight through the next unmarked intersection and you will soon arrive at the triangular intersection of Oregon Avenue, Nebraska Avenue, and Bingham Drive. There are various options but you will need to cross to the south side of Bingham Drive to pick up the Western Ridge Trail. Hike until you reach the dead end at the Horse Stable Road. Jog left and then pick up the trail via the gravel road that runs alongside the stables. At Oregon Avenue, the trail becomes paved and you follow it until the Rock Creek Park Nature Center. Look for the sign in the parking lot that indicates the Western Ridge Trail. Once you see Picnic Area #13, look for the pavilion and head towards it. From there, turn left and you'll see a tell-tale green blaze indicating you've found the trail once more. Continue hiking, diverging from the horse trail before meeting up with it once again and heading to Equitation Field. Just past this point, the trail splits once more; stay right. The trail grows hilly as you cross over Ridge Road and descend down a steep section. Once you reach Broad Branch Road, continue south until you pass Peirce Mill on your right. Pass under the Tilden Street Bridge and wrap around to the east until the trail ends at Bluff Bridge.

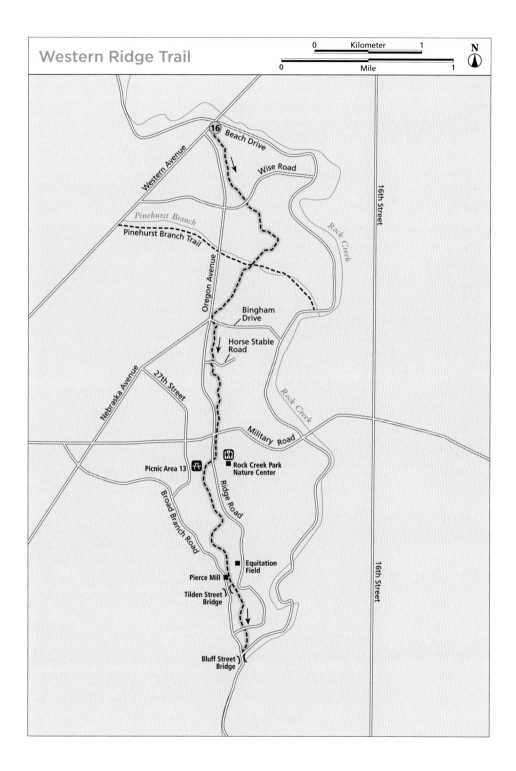

Western Ridge Trail

Kilometer
0 1

Mile
0 1

N

16 Beach Drive

Wise Road

Western Avenue

Pinehurst Branch

Pinehurst Branch Trail

Oregon Avenue

Rock Creek

16th Street

Bingham Drive

Horse Stable Road

Rock Creek

Nebraska Avenue

27th Street

Military Road

Picnic Area 13

Rock Creek Park Nature Center

Ridge Road

Broad Branch Road

Equitation Field

Pierce Mill

Tilden Street Bridge

16th Street

Bluff Street Bridge

MILES AND DIRECTIONS

0.0 Start at the "Welcome to Rock Creek Park" sign on Beach Drive.

0.5 Wise Road Intersection.

0.7 Unmarked intersection; stay straight.

0.9 Another unmarked intersection; stay straight.

1.1 Cross Pinehurst Branch before reaching the four-way intersection; stay straight.

1.3 Confusing intersection with two stacked green blazes; take a right.

1.4 Reach the intersection with Oregon Avenue, Nebraska Avenue, and Bingham Drive.

1.7 Horse Stable Road

1.9 Trail intersection; stay to the right.

2.2 Oregon Avenue and Military Road intersection.

2.3 Rock Creek Park Nature Center.

2.4 Picnic Area #13.

3.3 Arrive at Equitation Field.

3.6 Cross Ridge Road.

4.0 Encounter Peirce Mill on the right side.

4.5 You've reached Bluff Bridge and the end of your hike.

KALEN THORIEN
The Grand Sawtooth Loop
Stanley, Idaho

Kalen Thorien is a professional, four-season athlete, which is a rarity in the outdoor space. It started with a love of snow and a passion for skiing; shredding big-mountain powder was how she initially made her mark. But her interest in everything outdoors was omnipresent, and she soon grew a legion of fans based on her warm-weather endeavors: hiking, backpacking, packrafting, canyoneering, and Harley Davidson motorcycle riding. In 2015, she signed with Salomon as a four-season athlete, and it's been a wild ride ever since.

Kalen Thorien KALEN THORIEN

In addition to appearing in Warren Miller's *Line of Descent* film, Kalen also starred in multiple on-screen endeavors via her partnership with Salomon. In print, her work and accomplishments have been detailed in such publications as *National Geographic*, the *New York Times*, *Outside*, *Powder*, *ESPN*, and *Condé Nast Traveler*. You can follow along with her latest adventure via her wildly popular Instagram account: @KalenThorien.

The Grand Sawtooth Loop Trail contains some of the most beautiful scenery in Idaho. The loop is arguably the premiere trekking route in the state, swinging by some of the most magnificent sights. The trail has it all: color-infused lakes, river crossings, rugged ridgelines, and 360-degree views from mountain passes. It isn't a route meant for beginners, but if you want a small taste of Idaho wilderness, this is the best loop to tackle.

Nearest Town: Stanley, Idaho

Getting There: From Stanley, drive 35 miles northwest and south on ID 21. Then take a left (going east) on Forest Road #524 (or Grandjean Road). Follow the road for 7 miles. Then take a left on Forest Road #824 at the Sawtooth Lodge. You can catch the trail from the southeast corner of the campground.

Trailhead: Grandjean Campground **GPS:** N44 08.934', W115 09.022'

Fees and Permits: The Forest Service asks that all visitors to the Sawtooth Wilderness obtain a permit. If you are traveling in a group smaller than eight people, you can self-issue the permit at the trailhead. If your group is larger, you must obtain your permit from a Forest Service office. There is no charge.

Trail Users: Hikers, backpackers, trail runners

Elevation Gain: 10,265 feet

Length: 50 miles RT (loop)

Approximate Hiking Time: 4–6 Days

Difficulty: Strenuous

Insider Info: The Grand Sawtooth Loop has multiple iterations as various trails wrap through the area, allowing hikers to hop on or off the loop at multiple locations. If you don't have time for the 50-mile loop, consider shortening it for an abbreviated version of the hike.

Managing Agency: Sawtooth National Recreation Area

EXPERIENCING IT

It takes a lot to intimidate Kalen Thorien. This 29-year-old former wildland-firefighting, Harley-Davidson-driving, nomadic trailer-living woman is wildly fierce and unapologetically independent. She is a woman who knows how to suffer, but it wasn't always that way.

Kalen grew up outside of Boise, Idaho, and was anything but the quintessential outdoor darling, let alone a pro big mountain skier or four-season athlete. She laughs as she shares stories of feigning illness to avoid family ski trips to Bogus Basin, the nearby local hill. Instead, she opted for more traditional pursuits like ballet and viola lessons. But somewhere along the line, that all changed.

Upper Cramer Lake in all its majesty KALEN THORIEN

"My mom always encouraged me to be myself; I just had to figure out who that was," Kalen muses.

She began piecing it together in high school when she discovered her love for skiing. Instead of pretending to be sick to get out of family ski trips, Kalen began ditching class by forging her mother's checks to pay for day pass lift tickets. Skiing wasn't a talent that came easily and Kalen is quick to say that she needed to put in a lot of work and effort. In fact, by the time she graduated from high school, she was still unable to get down an entire black diamond ski run without eating a face full of snow.

But she persevered. Undaunted and fearless, she snagged her diploma, deferred college for one year, and packed up her life to move to Utah. Her destination: Alta Ski Area. Her goal: to become a ski bum.

Of course, ski bums usually know how to handle themselves on planks, so Kalen had a lot of work to do. Anytime she would see a female shredding down the hillside, she chased her down and asked how she was able to do whatever it was that impressed her so much. Eventually, she figured it out and, after a few seasons, began convincing local photographers to include her in ski-related photoshoots. In the summers, she hustled as a wildland firefighter, chasing quickly moving fire walls and leading predominantly male crews. It was a good way to enable her true passion—skiing—but it also taught her a helpful life lesson.

"I learned how to suffer when I was a firefighter," Kalen remembers. "I learned how to enjoy suffering."

But as Kalen spent more and more time in the Utah mountains that she grew to love—fighting fires in the summer and shredding powder fields in the winter—her ski career began to take off. Before she knew it, photographers were calling her to appear in their shoots; all her hard work and incessant nagging was paying dividends. These

Checking out the view at Alpine Lake KALEN THORIEN

Filling water at Upper Cramer Lake KALEN THORIEN

days, it's not unusual to see Kalen gracing the pages of any outdoor magazine; she nabbed the cover of *Powder* in 2012 and of *SKI* magazine in 2015.

But Kalen is more than just a pretty face and badass skier. There is something about Kalen's call-it-like-it-is personality that strikes a chord with her fans. She is real, and she doesn't sugarcoat anything for anyone. She won't pretend to have it all together, or even feign that she has just a piece.

Is it her sometimes-graphic language that hits a nerve with her supporters? Or perhaps it's the fact that she once called a 1993 Bigfoot trailer her permanent home as she bounced around outdoor locations in search of the next adventure? Maybe it's her willingness to get down 'n dirty and tinker with her new baby, a 1993 Harley Davidson FXR Super Glide motorcycle?

Regardless of what it is, Kalen gives off a tough mentality, so it is easy to forget that she too is human. And there is nothing like an overnight backpacking trip to remind you of your own mortality and sensitivity.

It was 2012 and Kalen embarked on her first-ever solo backpacking trip. She was a few nights into the Sawtooth Loop and opted to spend the evening at Upper Cramer Lake. She pitched her tent and began fixing a basic dinner on her compact backpacking stove when she heard branches crack in the brush behind her. Startled, Kalen glanced behind her to see rustling leaves and a persistent chaos in the shrubs. The cause of the movement was a mystery, but that didn't make much of a difference to Kalen. Something was out there.

Petrified, she grabbed her entire cookstove and hightailed it inside her tent, desperate for the protection of the flimsy nylon walls. The sun was still shining as it

Kalen hides out in her tent to avoid the mysterious sounds of nature. KALEN THORIEN

wasn't even close to sunset yet, but she didn't care: She was not coming out for the remainder of the evening. Instead, she finished cooking her meal in the vestibule—a completely ill-advised maneuver in bear country—and then climbed into her sleeping bag while wearing her headphones with music blasting as loud as she needed to completely drown out any semblance of noise from outside her tent. To improve on her make-believe world, she downed an entire bottle of wine she had packed in, hoping the combination of deafening tunes and major inebriation would help her forget that something large lurked in the bushes behind her. Eventually, she dozed off—or passed out—with Edward Abbey's *Desert Solitaire* resting against her chest and the obnoxiously loud tunes blasting from her headphones.

Morning arrived and it was as if the previous evening never happened. Kalen awoke early enough to shoot some sunrise photos, so she grabbed her camera and strolled out to the lake to witness one of the most glorious sunrises she had ever seen up until that point. As she watched the pinks and oranges streak across the sky and the warmth reflect against the surface of the water, she found herself questioning her behavior the night before. With the sun creeping up into the sky and her mind fresh and clear for the start of a new day, she thought to herself, *"What in the world was wrong with me last night?!"*

To this day, Kalen credits this particular night at Upper Cramer Lake with jump-starting her entire backpacking career. Since then, she has completed numerous off-trail, multi-night trips that make her solo overnight at Cramer look like amateur hour, but it will always be the place where she first experienced how grand Mother Nature truly can be.

THE HIKE

Beginning at the trailhead, you will soon cross a footbridge as it spans Trail Creek. Almost immediately after, you will reach a trail junction. This is the beginning of the loop and you should take a left if you are hiking it clockwise.

FOUR TIPS FOR YOUR FIRST SOLO BACKPACKING TRIP

If you want to embark upon your first solo backpacking trip, keep these tips in mind:

1. Make a solid plan—and tell others.
   Do your research ahead of time by studying maps and reading up on trip reports. If you know the area, you are less likely to run into issues.
2. Plan on failure.
   Let's be real: It is likely that something will go wrong. Maybe a tent pole will snap or you'll realize you forgot your extra base layer. If you have a few mistakes built into the game plan, you'll be able to rebound much easier.
3. Prepare for solitude.
   One of the toughest aspects for any first-timer is the feeling of utter solitude. That may sound silly since it is obviously what you signed up for, but backpacking alone can frequently feel like an echo chamber. Prepare yourself to be utterly and truly alone so that the sound of silence won't cause you alarm.
4. Don't panic if you get lost.
   On the outside chance you get lost on the trail, don't panic. Instead, stop and think. Have you seen any notable trail markers? Geological features? Look through your photos to see if anything is recognizable. If you really can't figure out where you are, sit down and stay awhile (after all, you have a tent!) Someone will find you soon.

The trail immediately begins switchbacking up a hillside full of dry grass that subtly transitions to lodgepole pines as you climb higher and higher. You will soon reach a series of rickety Trail Creek crosses that all use logs as bridges; exercise caution. Continue hiking, staying straight at the trail junction with Trail Creek Lakes, and then climb the short series of switchbacks until you reach a four-way junction. Bear right, eventually descending into a beautiful basin. This is known as the McGown Lakes. From here, ascend until you catch your first glimpse of Sawtooth Lake, the biggest alpine lake in the entire range. The route descends down to the lake and then wraps around the eastern shore before exiting at the southeast side. From here, continue straight through the junction and begin the long descent into the canyon of North Fork Baron Creek. You will know you've reached the bottom of the canyon once you reach an old burn area from the early 1990s. Cross the creek on logs and continue left at the next fork; if you go right, you'll return immediately to the trailhead.

Hike up the canyon from Baron Creek, winding through meadows filled with wildflowers if you time it right. Gently climb past Tohobit Falls; you will soon reach the base of Baron Creek Falls. Curve left and ascend a long series of switchbacks before the trail levels off and crosses another creek, climbing for the last time up to the shores of Baron Lake. Hike along the eastern shore for a short distance before first veering away from the lake up to Upper Baron Lake and then on to Baron Divide.

From the divide, you'll drop down until you reach the beautiful Alpine Lake. The trail is heavily used at this point and easy to follow as it traverses and then descends to Flat Rock Junction; this is where you meet the trail from Redfish Lake Creek. Turn right and cross Redfish Lake Creek before following alongside it, ascending up to Lower Cramer Lake and subsequently Middle and Upper Cramer Lakes. Above Upper Cramer Lake, the trail is lightly used as it ascends to a high pass. You will then descend a moderately steep slope as you drop down to the western shores of Hidden Lake. Below the lake, switchback through a forest down to a trail junction immediately after the South Fork Payette River. Take a right; you have a direct 19 miles back to your car.

MILES AND DIRECTIONS

0.0 Begin near the large sign and permit station at the east end of the parking lot at Grandjean Campground.

0.1 Cross the footbridge over Trail Creek.

0.2 Trail junction; take a left to complete the loop clockwise.

1.5 River crossing.

2.8 River crossing.

3.5 River crossing.

4.3 Trail junction; stay straight. The trail to the right goes to Trail Creek Lakes, a recommended side trip.

The Grand Sawtooth Loop

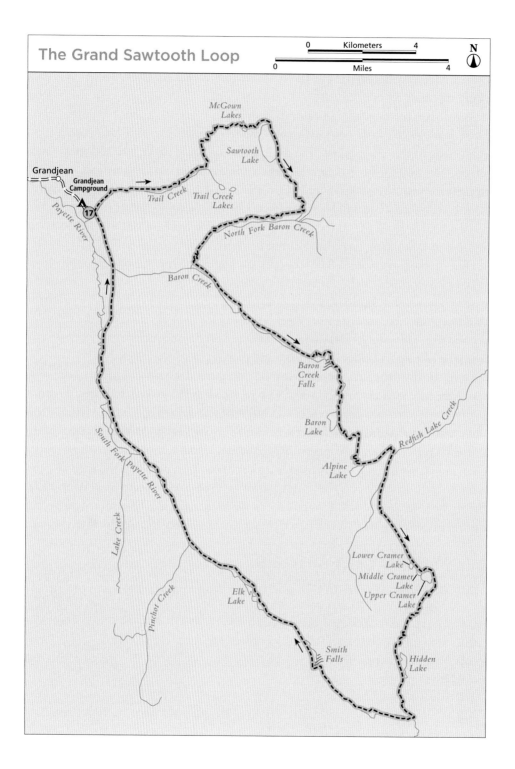

McGown
Lakes

Sawtooth
Lake

Grandjean

Grandjean
Campground

17

Payette River

Trail Creek

Trail Creek
Lakes

North Fork Baron Creek

Baron Creek

Baron
Creek
Falls

Baron
Lake

Redfish Lake Creek

South Fork Payette River

Alpine
Lake

Lake Creek

Lower Cramer
Lake

Middle Cramer
Lake

Upper Cramer
Lake

Pinchot Creek

Elk
Lake

Smith
Falls

Hidden
Lake

4.9 Four-way trail junction; bear right.

6.5 The first of the McGown Lakes.

7.8 You're temporarily done with climbing as you've reached the northern shore of Sawtooth Lake.

9.4 Pass by the eastern shores of two small ponds.

10.1 The trail turns sharply to the west.

12.8 River crossing.

13.8 Trail junction; stay straight to remain on the loop.

18.8 River crossing.

19.7 You've reached the eastern shores of Baron Lake.

21.9 The descent is almost over as you have reached Alpine Lake.

23.2 Trail junction; stay to the right.

26.3 You've reached Lower Cramer Lake, the smallest of the trio.

28.3 At almost 9,500 feet, you've reached the high point of the loop. It's all downhill from here!

29.2 River crossing.

30.0 You should catch your first glimpse of Hidden Lake from the hillside above its western shores.

31.4 Trail junction; stay right to hike the last 19-mile stretch.

32.5 Trail junction; stay straight.

34.5 Trail junction; take a right and catch a glimpse of the beautiful Smith Falls.

36.7 You've reached the eastern shores of Elk Lake. From here, you can take the trail all the way back to the parking lot.

18

MIRNA VALERIO

Chattooga River Trail
Clayton, Georgia

Mirna Valerio—aka the Mirnavator—is arguably one of the largest breakout stories in the twenty-first century's world of ultrarunning. To date, she has finished ten ultramarathons and nine marathons, authored a book, picked up a handful of sponsors,

and been named *National Geographic*'s 2018 Adventurer of the Year. And she did it all without winning a single race. Matter of fact, her goal is quite the opposite: Don't be last.

Mirna is a plus-sized runner whose aim is to spread a message of body positivity. The founder of the blog *Fat Girl Running*, she began her website in 2011 while training for her first marathon. Over time, the blog picked up traction but her story didn't explode until the *New York Times* wrote an article about her in 2015. From there, it was like dynamite. *Runner's World*, *Shape*, *Self Magazine*, ESPN, and *NBC Nightly News* all followed, lauding Mirna for her inspirational

Mirna Valerio MIRNA VALERIO

messaging regarding "fat fitness." In an era full of marketing jargon and social media hyperboles, Mirna's honesty is refreshing. "I'm good in my body," she says. "And I'll continue to insert my big butt into conversations to help others feel comfortable too."

Mirna is currently a public speaker and runner and is sponsored by Merrell, Swiftwick, and Skirt Sports.

Within two hours of Atlanta, the Chattooga River Trail continuously runs along the border between Georgia and South Carolina. Since the Chattooga River has been designated a National Wild and Scenic River by Congress, motorized vehicles aren't allowed within ¼ mile and facilities are limited. But this adds to the charm as hikers, trail runners, and kayakers are aplenty. While not on this particular section, the Chattooga River Trail's northern segment is known as "Waterfall Trail" thanks to the five cascades you can see within the last 15 miles.

Nearest Town: Clayton, Georgia

Getting There: From Clayton, take I-76 E for 9 miles. You will see the trailhead parking on the left side, on the west end of the US 76 bridge. You will park in Georgia, walk across the bridge, and pick up the trail in South Carolina.

Trailhead: Highway 76 Bridge Trailhead **GPS:** N34 48.852', W83 18.434'

Fees and Permits: None

Trail Users: Hikers, trail runners

Elevation Gain: 3,107 feet

Length: 19.1 miles (point-to-point)

Approximate Hiking Time: 1–2 Days

Difficulty: Moderate

Insider Info: The entire Chattooga River Trail is over 37 miles long and concludes at the North Carolina border, far beyond what this guide details. If you have the gumption, take 3–4 days to trek the entire trail while viewing scenery in three states.

Managing Agency: Chattahoochee National Forest

EXPERIENCING IT

For Mirna Valerio, the Chattooga River Trail is akin to the last 5 years of her life: tumultuous, exciting, and downright southern.

As a born-and-bred New Yorker (she was raised in Brooklyn), Mirna didn't think that anything could pull her away from her beloved New York. She even experimented with a brief stint in Maryland only to find herself stomping on the brakes before returning north. She was a Yankee, better suited for life north of the Mason-Dixon rather than the gently sloping terrain of the old-soul Appalachians. But life is predictably unpredictable. Change was inevitable and 2013 saw Mirna and her family packing up their belongings and moving to the North Georgia mountains where she had been offered a new position at a boarding school.

The transition was rocky with a very real adjustment period. The already stressful situation became exacerbated with a bizarre illness that threw yet another wrench into her new life. But Mirna is nothing if not an adaptable chameleon. Eventually, she settled into her new home, her new job, and her new way of living.

There is a slower pace in the South, a stillness in the air that sweetly invites you to sit on the front porch with some lemonade while watching the world spin around you.

Taking a quick breather to smile for the camera MIRNA VALERIO

A late fall passage of the Chattooga River Trail MIRNA VALERIO

At first, this gentle environment helped her find her feet figuratively. But eventually Mirna thought it was high time she found them literally. Her new home faced the eastern spine of the Appalachians so the predawn rays of sun frequently saw Mirna on her front porch, eyes toward the hillside almost as if she was gazing at her future. Because in a way, that's exactly what she was doing.

As a lifelong runner, it was easy for her to find her stride in Georgia. She started simple, seeking out basic paths that meandered through corn-colored meadows full

Enjoying a long run MIRNA VALERIO

of grazing cattle, each beast slowly chewing breakfast while lazily watching her as she jogged by during her life-affirming daily runs. She scaled cow gates and cattle guards—something she certainly never found in New York—and bit by bit, pushed herself outside of the box she had unknowingly constructed. Eventually, her burgeoning sense of adventure spilled over, asking for more. Eager to explore, Mirna took her runs to new locations and new terrain. She found the mountains.

The Appalachians aren't like mountains anywhere else in the world. First formed 480 million years ago when North America and Africa smashed into each other, the Appalachians once reached heights equal to the behemoth peaks of the Rockies or even the Alps. Alas, this super continent (known as Pangea) eventually split apart, leaving behind half eroded remains in its wake. We now call these remains the Appalachian Mountains.

These days, the range certainly isn't the largest in size, but it more than makes up for that with character. Mirna quickly discovered that Appalachia has an inordinate amount of personality hidden within the lush and thick tree canopies that cover the hillsides. Each mountain held a surprise for anyone who wished to seek it out. With an entire range at her doorstep, Mirna simply rolled out of bed, laced up her sneakers, and chose a mountain to investigate. Many of the peaks were rolling and gentle,

THE CONTROVERSY BEHIND A WILD AND SCENIC RIVER

The Chattooga River has long been hailed as the last wild river in the country, but many locals believe that magic disappeared in 1972 when the movie *Deliverance* was released. Before it hit theaters, only a few people trickled down to Southern Appalachia's toughest river, but then "*Deliverance* Fever" hit, and it hit hard thanks to the Chattooga River's role as the fictional Cahulawassee River in the film. The number of visitors quickly escalated into the tens of thousands, causing many locals to refer to the film as "the worst thing that ever happened to the river."

But then, on May 10, 1974, the Chattooga River was designated a Wild and Scenic River, the first river east of the Mississippi to earn such an accolade. Signed into law by President Lyndon B. Johnson on October 2, 1968, the National Wild and Scenic River Act designates that our country protect wild rivers from development that would significantly or detrimentally change their scenic nature. By 2018 (the 50-year anniversary of the law), over 12,700 miles along 208 rivers have been preserved, a statistic that pleases many environmentalists. However, this classification isn't without controversy.

In 1976, the U.S. Forest Service banned paddling in an effort to protect trout populations. As years rolled by, this ban greatly ruffled the feathers of the paddling community since the Chattooga was the only boat-friendly river in the Forest Service to ban paddling. In fact, in 2006 American Whitewater sued the Forest Service to reverse the paddling ban, arguing that the ban violated the Wild and Scenic Rivers act, which encourages recreational use. A U.S. District Court agreed, but through a series of appeals, the ban was not lifted until 2012. Finally, the Forest Service announced that boaters with permits could paddle the Upper Chattooga if water levels were high enough.

allowing Mirna to ease into her run with a gracious forgiveness that can only be found in the South. Some peaks felt demanding and relentless, unyielding by nature and uncomfortable by topography. Others still felt mysterious and challenging, constantly asking more of Mirna as she delved deeper into the mountainous region. She ran until she was tired and when she felt fatigued, she would walk. But she always kept moving as she explored more and more of her new neighborhood.

It was during one of these many runs that Mirna discovered the Chattooga River Trail.

Located just a hop, skip, and a quick run away from her new home, the Chattooga River Trail epitomized everything Mirna had grown to appreciate about life in the South. Like Mirna herself, the trail was pleasant and amiable with just a dash of sass. Her standard run became a 20-mile roundtrip voyage (10 miles out, 10 miles back) that amounted to just over 2,000 feet of elevation gain. It was enough elevation to challenge Mirna and contribute to her training, but truly it was more of a pleasant addition to the beautiful surroundings. The trail is lush and wet, frequently filled with brightly colored rhododendrons whose happy blooms stand on woody stems in stark contrast to the dense greenery covering the slopes. On damp mornings, the earthy smell of the spongy soil combined with the clean scent of the morning dew, creating a memorable assault on her senses as she journeyed down the path.

Mirna, enjoying an early autumn run MIRNA VALERIO

The trail also moves at a pace that Mirna associates with the South. There aren't any quad-busting climbs or knee-banging descents, and hikers certainly won't battle high altitude. Rather, the Chattooga River Trail meanders to and fro, wrapping around rolling hills and winding up and over forest-covered knobs, so thick with trees that the probably pleasant views are choked out by creeping vines and scattered leaves fitting together over the exposed sky, like puzzle pieces on a coffee table. It's the perfect trail to be one with your thoughts as you catch occasional glimpses of the Chattooga River in all its glory, babbling around the bend with ecstatic groups of kayakers caught amidst the frothing waves.

It became the default trail for Mirna in her early southern years, the trail she would reliably visit whenever she wanted to log some miles. It was consistent and steadfast, and she continued to run its comfortable curves through all of her life's journeys: when the *New York Times* article published, before speaking with *Runner's World*, and whenever she needed to get out and find some nature.

These days, southern living is in Mirna's rearview mirror as she has once again relocated to the North. But still, when asked to choose any single trail in the entire country, Mirna immediately opted for the Chattooga River Trail. After all, she always knew she could rely on the Chattooga River.

THE HIKE

Once on the actual trail, follow the bright green blazes to guide you along the way. Almost immediately, you gradually climb from the trailhead, the lowest point (1,110 feet) of the entire length. Cross a wooden bridge and ignore any side trails you encounter within the first mile; you want to stay on the main path. Continue hiking as the trail winds away from the river; you won't reach the water again until Mile 4. From there, the trail once again turns away from the Chattooga River to climb up and over a few rolling hills before returning to the river just before Mile 6; you will stay along the water for 1.5 miles. After 10 miles, the Chattooga River Trail merges with the Bartram Trail and you will hike along them both until this segment's terminus at the Russell Bridge (GA 28 Bridge).

MILES AND DIRECTIONS

0.0 From the parking area in Georgia on the west side of the US 76 bridge, walk across the bridge and pick up the path at the trailhead in South Carolina.

0.5 Trek across the small wooden bridge.

0.7 Cross Pole Creek.

1.3 Come to a nice, small waterfall.

2.9 Pass a small trailside campsite.

4.1 Near the Chattooga River once again.

6.0 After trekking away from the river, you reach the river once more. This is a great place to fill up water if needed.

6.5 Trail intersects with Licklog Trail; stay straight.

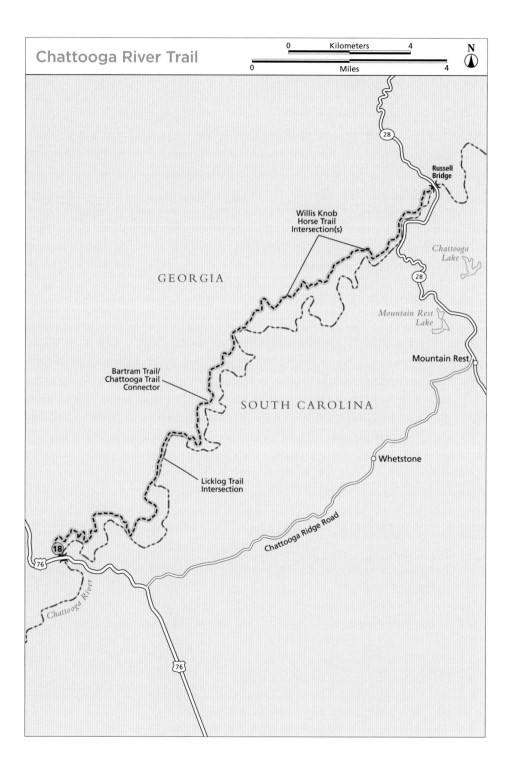

Chattooga River Trail

7.4 Trail turns left through a series of switchbacks up the hillside.

8.4 The path splits; stay to the right.

10.0 The Chattooga River Trail merges to the right with the Bartram Trail.

10.3 The path splits; stay to the left.

16.6 The trail intersects with Willis Knob Horse Trail; stay straight.

17.3 The path splits; stay to the right.

18.0 Just after a stream crossing, the path splits again; stay to the right.

19.1 Reach Russell Bridge (GA 28 Bridge).

JOLIE VARELA

Methuselah National Recreation Loop Trail Big Pine, California

Jolie Varela is a Paiute and Tule River Yokut from Payahüünadü (the place of flowing waters). Today, her homeland is more commonly known as California's Owens Valley. In 2017, Jolie founded Indigenous Women Hike (@IndigenousWomenHike), an

Jolie Varela MARIAH L. DAVID

Instagram platform and movement designed to encourage more indigenous people (specifically the youth) to reconnect with their land.

Personally, Jolie hasn't always been interested in the outdoors, and it wasn't until a few years ago that she discovered her love for hiking. While dealing with depression, she began using solo hiking as a coping mechanism and realized how beneficial it was for her mental wellness. In the process, she pondered all of the historical traumas that presently deter indigenous people from hitting the trail. She decided she wanted to be part of the solution. As a result, Indigenous Women Hike was formed. She then opted to take it one step further and in August 2018 put together an all-female hike of the John Muir Trail—only she didn't call it that. Instead, she and the eleven other indigenous women dubbed the voyage the Nüümü Poyo, or the People's Trail. In speaking with her tribe's elders, she learned that the Nüümü Poyo was largely an ancestral trade route for her people. Under the American Indian Religious Freedom Act of 1978, she and the other women did not obtain any permits. Instead, they embarked on the hike to retrace their ancestors' paths in an effort to empower the country's indigenous people and highlight their connection with Mother Earth.

The Methuselah National Recreation Loop Trail is in the Ancient Bristlecone Pine Forest portion of the White Mountains. Situated between 10,000 and 11,000 feet, this hike isn't the most topographically difficult but more than makes up for that with its call for high-altitude lungs. As an added bonus, one of the oldest trees in the world exists in this loop in the Methuselah Grove. Park officials intentionally keep its identity secret for fear of bandits chopping down or otherwise destroying the tree, but simply knowing it exists on the trail gives hikers plenty of reason to ponder their existence in this vast universe.

Nearest Town: Big Pine, California

Getting There: From Big Pine, drive east on CA 168 for just over 12 miles. Turn left on White Mountain Road. Drive another 10 miles before taking a right to the Schulman Grove Visitor Center. You will see a sign for the trail.

Trailhead: Methuselah National Recreation Loop Trailhead **GPS:** N37 23.128', W118 10.721'

Fees and Permits: $3/person or maximum $6 per car. It is free if you already have a National Parks Pass.

Trail Users: Hikers, trail runners

Elevation Gain: 610 feet

Length: 3.7 miles RT (loop)

Approximate Hiking Time: Half Day

Difficulty: Easy–Moderate

Insider Info: Stop by the Visitor Center before hiking to pick up a brochure ($1). Bring this on the hike to coordinate with the numbered signposts along the trail to learn tidbits of information about the trees and their surroundings.

Managing Agency: Inyo National Forest

EXPERIENCING IT

Perched high above Payahüünadü on a windswept ridge lives an isolated grove of bristlecone pine trees. Oxygen is scarce above 10,000 feet but the bristlecone doesn't mind. In fact, it prefers the core-shaking winds and blustery temperatures that blow in with a ferocity very few trees can withstand. Bristlecones do not appear to be the toughest lot but they've won the battle of survival of the fittest by thriving in this otherworldly environment.

Their gnarled limbs are equal parts delightful and nightmarish as they twist and contort in various directions, stretching away from their core almost as if their arms

Colorful striations on the trunk MARIAH L. DAVID

are reaching outwards and upwards towards the sky. You can never predict the shape of the pines; some are girthy and squat like a sumo wrestler while others grow long and lean, as twisted and wiry as a corkscrew. But as arthritic and wizened as the limbs appear, they are shockingly smooth to the touch. Thanks to the turbulent winds, pebbles and ice constantly grind against the bark, creating a smooth glass-like surface that is as polished as an ice rink after it sees a Zamboni.

The harsh conditions seemingly slow the growth of these ancient trees, but that is likely a good thing. Bristlecones grow fearfully slow; some years, they don't even add a single growth ring to their trunk, and it may take 100 years for the tree to expand one inch in diameter. They are deceptive in that regard, for it is not rare to observe a seemingly tiny sapling only to realize it is actually hundreds of years old. But this painstakingly slow maturation process is also the secret to the bristlecone's longevity, creating an incredibly dense and stout trunk that can withstand any of life's hardships. Bugs and fungi cannot even begin to penetrate these powerful trees and it is possible to see a dead bristlecone standing upright for centuries, resisting rot in favor of petrification.

Buried within the depths of the Methuselah National Recreation Loop Trail lives one of the most celebrated bristlecones of them all: Methuselah. Named after the biblical patriarch who lived to be 969 years old, the arboreal Methuselah was once believed to be the oldest non-clonal organism on Earth at a whopping 4,850 years old. To put that in perspective, Methuselah was alive—albeit a sapling—when the

Bristlecone pines are one of the hardiest trees in existence. Mariah L. David

pyramids of Egypt were built. Since then, however, a more senior bristlecone has been discovered, making Methuselah the playful younger sibling. But that doesn't take away from the mystique of this magical tree. Since its specific identity is a well-kept secret, no one can accurately discern which tree is the namesake of Methuselah Grove. Instead, hikers of this loop merely stop and stand in wonder, pondering their own humanity against the perceived far-reaching immortality of these glorious trees. The mystery is part of the trail's charm.

In some ways, Jolie Varela likes to think of herself as a bristlecone pine, too.

As an indigenous woman whose ancestor history reaches back farther than Methuselah, Jolie is inexplicably tied to Payahüünadü and Payahupaway (Bishop) through roots deeper than the bristlecones themselves. She grew up in Payahüünadü as did many generations prior to her; her family's heritage flows from the White Mountains down into the valley and has existed in that geographical area for longer than most history books can detail. While some outdoor enthusiasts look at the Methuselah Walk and the ancient bristlecones as another outdoor experience to notch on their belt, Jolie views it as a sacred aspect of her familial history. The bristlecone's longstanding roots represent the roots of her people, too.

Jolie audibly grimaces as she tells of a time that a staff member at the Schulman Grove Visitor Center explained to her how indigenous people never journeyed up that direction since they did not have any use for the bristlecone trees. Although it isn't in any literature than can be found at the center or elsewhere, Jolie's elders share many stories about her people going up into the White Mountains and gathering pine nuts in that area as a means of sustenance. Harvesting and gathering pine nuts is a laborious process but her people routinely undertook the task.

Today, Jolie still continues the pine nut tradition. Of course, various types of pine nuts are readily available at any grocery store, but she prefers to respect and acknowledge her ties to the land while celebrating the traditions of her people. In fact, Jolie

Jolie hikes along a barren section of the trail. MARIAH L. DAVID

PROMETHEUS

Until 2013, Methuselah was thought to be the oldest tree in the world. As we now know, another (unnamed) bristlecone was subsequently discovered that outdated Methuselah and has since taken the crown for the eldest tree around. But prior to this discovery existed a tree named Prometheus.

In 1964, Donald Rusk Currey was a graduate student at the University of North Carolina at Chapel Hill studying climate dynamics of the Little Ice Age using tree-ring dating techniques. He became aware of the Great Basin bristlecone pine population, not realizing scientists had already examined that area. He analyzed some of the trees and based on their size and growth patterns, he became convinced there were some very old specimens in his midst. He began taking core samples and found some trees that were more than 3,000 years old. Specifically, he became interested in a tree he named WPN-114, or Prometheus.

Currey tried at least four times with a 28-inch borer, but was unable to obtain a series of overlapping cores, even going as far as breaking two borers and getting one stuck in the process. Finally, he requested permission from the U.S. Forest Service to fell the tree so that he could examine the entire trunk in cross-section. Donald E. Cox, a district Forest Service ranger, felt that Currey's request was scientifically sound and after convincing his superiors that WPN-114 was not significant, gained permission to chop it down. The tree was subsequently cut and sectioned, with various sections hauled out for analysis by Currey and then others. To his surprise, it was the oldest tree ever discovered at that point in time. If alive today, it would be 4,898 years old, roughly 50 years older than Methuselah.

This tragic series of events did lead to a positive outcome. As a result, Great Basin National Park was created and tighter restrictions were put on felling trees. This is also one of the reasons it was decided to keep the identity of Methuselah a secret for future generations.

has even discovered grinding stones on the trail while hiking, evidence that her ancestors visited that very area. When she finds these grinding stones, she likes to sit and imagine the scene as it unfolded, with her great-great-great grandmother grinding the nuts against the rocks in preparation for feeding her people. This is history; this is her history; this is the land's history.

In her spare time, Jolie likes to head up to the Methuselah National Recreation Loop Trail, admiring the view of the Eastern Sierra all the while. And when she is on the trail, she immerses herself in the deep history that emanates from the shallow roots of the ancient trees surrounding her. She breathes in the brisk air high above the valley floor and imagines her people doing the same thing thousands of years ago. Perhaps those same trees were standing there, protecting her ancestors too.

THE HIKE

Starting on the edge of the parking lot, follow the sign for "Methusalah Walk." There will be a slight dip at first but then you will begin climbing. Fairly quickly, you will encounter a sign asking you to stay to the right; the left trail is where you will close the loop upon your return hike. Continue hiking upward until you reach the high point of the trail; you will see a bench indicating you are at the summit. Take the time to admire the views!

From the bench, the trail turns south. Shortly thereafter, you will see the trail junction with Cabin Trail; stay straight to maintain the Methuselah National Recreation Loop Trail. The trail now begins to descend, eventually turning back east as you continually hike downward. You will soon hike into an area known as the Sculpture Garden, where harsh weather, wind, and ice have molded the bristlecone pines into unique and varied shapes. Continue hiking well onto the backside of the loop, passing through Methuselah Grove, home of one of the oldest trees in the world. After the grove you will hit the lowest point on the trail, from which you will climb out until you reach the trailhead from whence you came.

The sun peeks through the trees. MARIAH L. DAVID

Methuselah National Recreation Loop Trail

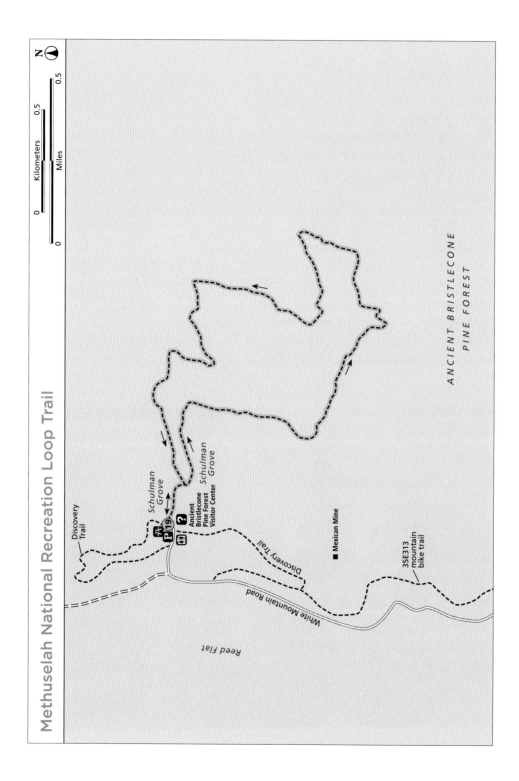

Discovery Trail

Schulman Grove

Schulman Grove

Ancient Bristlecone Pine Forest Visitor Center

White Mountain Road

Discovery Trail

Reed Flat

■ Mexican Mine

35E313 mountain bike trail

ANCIENT BRISTLECONE PINE FOREST

Kilometers
0   0.5

Miles
0   0.5

N

MILES AND DIRECTIONS

0.0 Start in the parking lot of the Schulman Grove Visitor Center.

0.2 Reach the sign asking you to stay to the right.

0.5 You've topped out at the high point of the trail.

0.8 The junction with the Cabin Trail; stay straight.

1.4 The trail turns east.

2.3 You've reached the Sculpture Garden.

2.4 Now you will enter Methuselah Grove.

2.8 The low point on the trail.

3.7 You are back in the parking lot.

PAMELA ZOOLALIAN

Tuolumne Meadows to Devils Postpile
Yosemite Valley, California

Pamela Zoolalian is an extreme sports enthusiast who specialized in street luge and downhill skateboarding in the mid 1990s. As one of the few women in these male-dominated sports, she was the only female athlete to qualify and compete in ESPN's

Pamela Zoolalian PAMELA ZOOLALIAN

X Games, NBC's Gravity Games, and the Playstation Extreme Games. In fact, she was so prolific in her sports that her leathers, helmet, and street luge board were displayed at Disney's All Star Café in Orlando.

Additionally, Pamela was a commentator within the skating industry, appearing in coverage for the Gravity Games, X Games, and the Vans Triple Crown. She hosted her own radio show called *The Core Radio*, and was even featured in a Nike commercial as the Just Do It Downhill Diva. Pamela was also photographed by Annie Leibovitz for her *Women in Sports Project*.

This particular stretch of the John Muir Trail is unique in that you reap the rewards of the iconic Yosemite National Park, but you begin in a much quieter section of the popular park by starting this leg in Tuolumne Meadows. From there, hike up and over Donohue Pass and drop into the Ansel Adams Wilderness, named after the renowned photographer who was captivated by its beauty. Hikers pass by the famous Thousand Island Lake, one of the more beautiful alpine lakes in the Eastern Sierra.

Nearest Town: Yosemite Valley, California

Getting There: From Yosemite Valley in Yosemite National Park, take CA 120 for 10 miles until you come to the Crane Flat turnoff onto Tioga Road. Then take Tioga Road 38 miles east until you come upon the meadows. If you arrive in the park from the east entrance at Tioga Pass, simply take Tioga Road west 8 miles and you will see the meadows.

Trailhead: Tuolumne Meadows **GPS:** N37 52.616', W119 20.752'

Fees and Permits: Yosemite wilderness permits are required ($5 per confirmed reservation + $5 per person) for overnight stays in the park. These are available through a lottery system that starts 168 days prior to the start date of your trip. Additionally, hikers exiting Yosemite via Donohue Pass need to also apply for a Donohue Pass exit quota.

Trail Users: Hikers, backpackers, trail runners

Elevation Gain: 4,967 feet

Length: 35 miles (point-to-point)

Approximate Hiking Time: 3–4 Days

Difficulty: Strenuous

Insider Info: This portion of trail wraps through the Ansel Adams Wilderness and passes the practically famous Thousand Island Lake. This aptly named body of water is dotted with small islands and affords an amazing view of Banner Peak. If you can swing it, I highly recommend spending a night—or two!—here to enjoy the scenery. ***Note:*** Mosquitoes can be especially vicious if you arrive near the hatch (typically around July, but it depends on the year's snow pack), so plan accordingly.

Managing Agency: Yosemite National Park; Inyo National Forest

View of Cathedral Peak Pamela Zoolalian

EXPERIENCING IT

The first two-thirds of Pamela Zoolalian's life revolved around speed. As an outdoorsy girl growing up with California's Angeles National Park as her backyard, she did not understand the concept of fear. She splashed in creeks and played with tadpoles; she ran through the forest and regularly skinned her knees. Her life was outside and as a result, it never occurred to her to be scared of much. Life was full of adventure and its consequences; that was all she knew and what she loved. Whether she realized it then or not, this was a personality trait that would serve her well later in life.

Pamela was gutsy and her stubborn streak only widened as she reached her 20s. Thanks to her fearlessness, she found friendship with an athletic group of guys, most of whom were professional athletes. They admired her perseverance and determination and never treated her any differently because she was a female. In fact, they respected her ability to decode any given situation and enjoyed challenging her by presenting her with more and more difficult tasks. She thrived under their tutelage and pushed her skill sets to new levels. There was no room for error and Pamela understood that every obstacle was a solvable problem. If she practiced enough and carefully observed her friends, she knew she was capable of anything.

It was this confidence and resolution that led her to street luge. Similar to the ice luge you now see in the Winter Olympic Games, street luge was just breaking onto the scene in the mid-90s and people were enamored with the high-risk nature of the sport. Participants rode a street luge board (similar to a long skateboard) in a supine position while bombing downhill at very high speeds, using the weight of their bodies to turn when needed. If they needed to stop, they used their feet, burning through a pair of outsoles daily. It was dangerous, thrilling, and packed full of speed. In short, it was the perfect sport for Pamela.

Around this same time, ESPN realized they were missing out on a burgeoning and profitable market: extreme sports. To remedy this, the network spent $10 million to launch the first-ever X Games in 1995, drawing 200,000 extreme sports athletes to the event in Rhode Island. Network executives cherry picked the most extreme games they could find to showcase at that first event; street luge was one of them.

Pamela remembers watching the first X Games on television and marveling at the insane 60-mph speeds of the street luge athletes. After the competition concluded, she and her friend immediately headed out to the nearest Home Depot for plywood, tubing, and 2×4 wood. Once she constructed her makeshift board, she experienced her first street luge run. It was 2 a.m., likely illegal, and Pamela was hooked.

Street luge came naturally to her. She possessed an uncanny ability to slow time down in her mind so that she could methodically and logically process any given situation, regardless of where she was or what she was doing. She learned to control the jitter-inducing adrenaline that is inherent in any extreme sport and compartmentalized

Morning view overlooking Virginia Lake PAMELA ZOOLALIAN

her fear. Instead, she harnessed that vibrancy and power to use in her favor. Her rational mindset gave her the best-available options while on the course, but her massive power aided her with speed. More than any sport prior, it was love at first ride.

But it was a male-dominated sport. Since women weigh much less than men, they competed at a major disadvantage, a fact that scared many females away from even trying. Pamela was a lone wolf surrounded by male competitors, but she didn't let that phase her. In fact, she approached it logically and rationally, just like she did everything else in life. Her tough mentality impressed her competitors once again, and she soon found them helping her. One built her a new board while another placed her on his team. These instances afforded her the opportunity to learn from professionals and improve her riding style. As a result, her skills shot through the roof—and the helpful camaraderie quickly dwindled. Instead of being helpful, the guys grew competitive, not wanting to be bested by one of the few females in the sport. Pamela took it all in stride, thriving on the competition.

Street luge took Pamela all over the globe at a time when the sport was bursting with popularity. As her skills increased so did the accolades. At one point, Pamela was the only female athlete to qualify and compete in street luge in the X Games, the NBC Gravity Games, and the Playstation Extreme Games.

As tends to happen with extreme sports, Pamela eventually grew away from street luge and found herself involved in other projects. She developed a skatewear line for women that did quite well, but when the economy crashed in 2008 her business struggled. In 2011 she closed her doors, unsure of what was next. It was a small industry

Timberline Lake PAMELA ZOOLALIAN

and gossip thrived, so Pamela made a scary decision to completely walk away from it all. She loved skating and street luge but her passions were now emotionally exhausting. She needed a change, and opted for one that was about as polar-opposite from street luge as any one sport could be: backpacking.

She set her sights on the John Muir Trail, the 212-mile journey that stretches from Yosemite National Park to the summit of Mt. Whitney. Backpacking was far slower and more methodical than any of her previous adrenaline-filled sports, but its calming nature was exactly why it appealed to her. Pamela spent 9 months preparing for the trek, carefully dehydrating meals and counting calories to stash in food resupply caches. She reviewed gear, cautiously choosing the best items for her adventure. She tirelessly trained, hiking 5 or 6 days each week under a heavy backpack, determined to strengthen her hiking muscles. It was often tedious work, but the absolute involvement

Looking down at the vertical climb up the Cables on Half Dome, an additional offshoot hike
PAMELA ZOOLALIAN

and reliance on planning helped her get away from the madness she had left behind in the skating world.

Pamela gave herself 30 days on the John Muir Trail. Other than a small sketchbook and a camera, she carried nothing to distract her: no music, no books, and no earphones. Instead, she focused on her experience, whatever it happened to be at any given moment. She didn't want a playlist packed with enthusiastic tunes to interrupt this experience that she intentionally set aside for clarification and mental restoration. She needed to be alone with her thoughts. She needed this time to move forward with her life.

And it worked. The month Pamela spent on the John Muir Trail was arguably the most therapeutic experience of her life. Everything was so simple. She awoke

WHAT IS THE JOHN MUIR TRAIL?

To many, the John Muir Trail is the premiere hiking trail in the United States. The 211-mile route runs along the spine of the Sierra Range between Yosemite National Park and Mt. Whitney (14,505 feet), the tallest peak in the lower 48. While the trail has indigenous origins (*See:* Jolie Varela chapter) that should not be forgotten, most people know it as the John Muir Trail, named after the iconic founder of the Sierra Club. John Muir's loud and proud style of advocating laid the groundwork for conserving much of the terrain spread throughout Yosemite, Kings Canyon, and Sequoia National Parks.

The entire route covers almost 47,000 feet of elevation gain throughout its 211 miles, and most of the trail is situated in designated wilderness. Over a third of the trail sits above 10,000 feet, affording thru-hikers and backpackers some of the most panoramic views in the lower 48. In the past, the trail was known for its relative solitude, but recent years have seen an influx in thru-hikers, leading to such precautionary measures as the Donohue Pass exit quota previously mentioned in the permit section.

Sunset at Thousand Island Lake WILL ROCHFORT

in the same tent every morning and ate basic meals, never fretting about too many choices because they simply weren't available. She walked when she felt like walking; she slept when she was tired. If she was hungry, she ate some food and if her feet hurt, she removed her shoes. She laughed and joked with other thru-hikers when she felt extroverted and kept to herself when she wanted solitude. Her time on the John Muir Trail was very simple but the clear-cut instructions and minimalistic nature of the thru-hike were actually what she needed at such a complicated time in her life.

Completing the John Muir Trail helped Pamela find the clarity she so desperately needed. In choosing to hike alone, she allowed herself the time and space she needed to ruminate on her identity. Who was she? What was important to her? Where did she go from here?

The John Muir Trail taught Pamela to walk her own walk, both on the trail and back in Los Angeles. She returned to the city and immediately became a National Ski Patrol member. Then she began teaching a travel course for the Sierra Club. Having walked away from such a transformative experience, Pamela wanted to better equip others to do the same. Thru-hiking changed the course of her life, and she understood its metamorphic powers more than most. Nature became her healer, and she aimed to help others find this same salve. Because everyone needs to walk their own walk at some point.

Beautiful views of Banner Peak at Thousand Island Lake WILL ROCHFORT

THE HIKE

Fortunately, this is a very easy trail to follow and will require minimal guidance. From the Tuolumne Meadows Wilderness Center, head south on the John Muir Trail section of the Pacific Crest Trail. You will follow John Muir Trail signs the entire way. Continue heading south as the trail remains relatively flat for the first 10 miles. This makes a great warm-up as you can prepare for the climbs you will face in the coming days. There are many options for campsites, but many choose to spend the first evening along Lyell Fork, opting to tackle Donohue Pass on the morning of the second day.

From Lyell Fork, you will begin steeply ascending, gaining almost 1,100 feet over the next 3.5 miles. Once you reach the top of Donohue Pass (11,056 feet), take a moment to catch your breath and admire the view. Looking south, you will see the Ansel Adams Wilderness in all of its glory; this is your target.

Descend Donohue Pass, gradually hiking downhill for the next 3 miles. When you reach the trail junction with Rush Creek Trail, continue straight to stay on the John Muir Trail. Shortly thereafter, you will gradually ascend once more, this time to the summit of Island Pass. It's easy to miss since it is a large summit, but keep your eyes peeled for amazing views of the Minarets to the west.

From there, you will quickly reach Thousand Island Lake on your right, shortly followed by Garnet Lake. Both make great campsites if you can schedule accordingly. A short-but-steep climb welcomes you after Garnet, but you are then rewarded with a gradual downhill for the next few miles so you can relax and enjoy the scenery. The trail rolls up and then down one more time by Shadow Lake before descending to Devils Postpile. As you near the national monument, you will encounter a few trail junctions, so be sure to stay on the John Muir Trail every time.

Note: In high season, you cannot leave a car at Devil's Postpile. If you opt for this point-to-point hike, you will need to take the $7 shuttle from the national monument to Mammoth Ski Resort. You can take Yosemite Area Regional Transportation System (YARTS) from Mammoth back to Yosemite.

MILES AND DIRECTIONS

0.0 Begin at the Tuolumne Meadows Wilderness Center. From here, head south and connect with the John Muir section of the Pacific Crest Trail.

1.1 Trail junction; stay right on the John Muir Trail.

2.2 Trail junction; stay straight.

4.2 Stream crossing.

6.6 Trail junction; stay straight on the John Muir Trail.

9.4 Stream crossing.

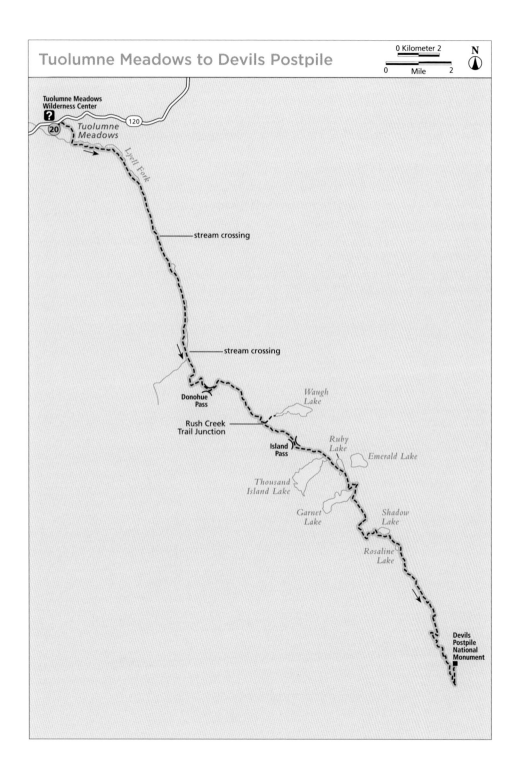

Tuolumne Meadows to Devils Postpile

0 Kilometer 2

0 Mile 2

N

Tuolumne Meadows
Wilderness Center

120

20

*Tuolumne
Meadows*

Lyell Fork

stream crossing

stream crossing

Donohue
Pass

*Waugh
Lake*

Rush Creek
Trail Junction

Island
Pass

*Ruby
Lake*

Emerald Lake

*Thousand
Island Lake*

*Garnet
Lake*

*Shadow
Lake*

*Rosaline
Lake*

Devils
Postpile
National
Monument

9.8 You've reached a great campsite along Lyell Fork.

10.0 Begin ascending Donohue Pass.

13.9 You've now reached the summit of Donohue, so enjoy the views.

17.5 Trail junction with Rush Creek Trail; stay straight and do not go to Waugh Lake.

20.8 You've now arrived at Thousand Island Lake; congrats!

23.9 Cross the bridge at the eastern end of Garnet Lake. The large stone slabs beneath the bridge make for a great place to relax and eat lunch.

25.0 Steeply descend via a series of switchbacks.

27.1 Trail junction; stay left to head toward Shadow Lake.

28.0 You are now on the southern shore of Shadow Lake.

29.7 Hike along the eastern shore of Rosalie Lake.

33.3 You will soon see the sign announcing your entrance to Devils Postpile National Monument.

35.0 You've reached the end of your trek. Catch a shuttle to Mammoth Ski Resort to return to Yosemite National Park.

Index

About the Author

Heather Balogh Rochfort is a freelance writer and author of *Backpacking 101*. Her website, *Just a Colorado Gal*, has been voted one of the top five best hiking and outdoor travel blogs by *USA Today*. She is also a gear writer for *Backpacker Magazine* and regularly appears on-air to discuss outdoor topics for the Weather Channel. An enthusiastic hiker, backcountry skier, backpacker, and trail runner, she lives outside of Denver with her husband, baby girl, and lovable yet geriatric mutt.